T0293251

The Rise and Fall of the Italian Economy

Carlo Bastasin and Gianni Toniolo provide a much-needed, up-to-date economic history of Italy from unification in 1861 to the present day. They show how, thirty years after unification, Italy began a long phase of convergence with more advanced economies so that by the late twentieth century Italy's per capita income reached the levels of Germany, France and the UK. From the mid-1990s, however, the Italian economy declined first in relative and then absolute terms. The authors describe the intertwined financial and institutional crises that eroded trust in the political system and in the economy at the exact juncture when new technologies and markets transformed the global economy. Long-standing problems of uneven levels of education and obsolete bureaucratic and judicial practices deepened the division between economically vibrant regions and the rest, causing polarization, political instability and rising public debt. Italy's contemporary malaise makes the country a test case for understanding the implications of protracted declines in productivity and the flattening of GDP growth for the stability of western democracies, resulting in populism, mistrust and political instability.

CARLO BASTASIN is Senior Fellow and Professor of European Economic Governance at the LUISS University in Rome and non-resident Senior Fellow at the Brookings Institution in Washington.

GIANNI TONIOLO was Senior Fellow at LUISS University School of European Political Economy, Professor Emeritus of Economics and History at Duke University and Research Fellow at the Centre for Economic Policy Research.

NEW APPROACHES TO ECONOMIC AND SOCIAL HISTORY

SERIES EDITORS

Marguerite Dupree (University of Glasgow)
Debin Ma (London School of Economics and Political Science)
Larry Neal (University of Illinois, Urbana-Champaign)

New Approaches to Economic and Social History is an important new text-book series published in association with the Economic History Society. It provides concise but authoritative surveys of major themes and issues in world economic and social history from the post-Roman recovery to the present day. Books in the series are by recognized authorities operating at the cutting edge of their field with an ability to write clearly and succinctly. The series consists principally of single-author works – academically rigorous and groundbreaking – which offer comprehensive, analytical guides at a length and level accessible to advanced school students and undergraduate historians and economists.

A full list of titles published in the series can be found at: www.cambridge.org/ newapproacheseconomicandsocialhistory.

The Rise and Fall of the Italian Economy

CARLO BASTASIN
LUISS University

GIANNI TONIOLO †
Duke University

CAMBRIDGE
UNIVERSITY PRESS

Shaftesbury Road, Cambridge CB2 8EA, United Kingdom

One Liberty Plaza, 20th Floor, New York, NY 10006, USA

477 Williamstown Road, Port Melbourne, VIC 3207, Australia

314–321, 3rd Floor, Plot 3, Splendor Forum, Jasola District Centre,
New Delhi – 110025, India

103 Penang Road, #05–06/07, Visioncrest Commercial, Singapore 238467

Cambridge University Press is part of Cambridge University Press & Assessment,
a department of the University of Cambridge.

We share the University's mission to contribute to society through the pursuit of
education, learning and research at the highest international levels of excellence.

www.cambridge.org
Information on this title: www.cambridge.org/9781009235341

DOI: 10.1017/9781009235303

First published 2023

A catalogue record for this publication is available from the British Library.

Library of Congress Cataloging-in-Publication Data
Names: Bastasin, Carlo, 1959– author. | Toniolo, Gianni, 1942– author.
Title: The rise and fall of the Italian economy / Carlo Bastasin, Libera Università
   Internazionale degli Studi Sociali Guido Carli, Roma, Gianni Toniolo, Duke
   University, North Carolina.
Description: 1 Edition. | New York, NY : Cambridge University Press, 2023. |
   Series: Naes new approaches to economic and social history | Includes bibliographical
   references.
Identifiers: LCCN 2023011777 (print) | LCCN 2023011778 (ebook) |
   ISBN 9781009235341 (hardback) | ISBN 9781009235310 (paperback) |
   ISBN 9781009235303 (epub)
Subjects: LCSH: Italy–Economic conditions–1945- | Italy–Economic conditions–
   1918–1945. | Italy–Economic conditions–1870-1918. | Italy–Economic policy. |
   Italy–History. | Italy–Politics and government.
Classification: LCC HC305 .B37273 2023 (print) | LCC HC305 (ebook) |
   DDC 330.945–dc23/eng/20230515
LC record available at https://lccn.loc.gov/2023011777
LC ebook record available at https://lccn.loc.gov/2023011778

ISBN 978-1-009-23534-1 Hardback
ISBN 978-1-009-23531-0 Paperback

Contents

Figures

Tables

Preface

This brief history of the Italian economy originates from a question: What happened to the economy that between 1890 and 1990 had caught up with the income and productivity levels of the most advanced countries in the world and then suddenly stopped growing at the end of the twentieth century?

The book finds that the relationship between political uncertainty, financial instability and economic growth is crucial to the functioning of a democratic society. We identify Italy's loss of confidence in itself in the early 1990s when a series of distinct crises, which had been building for many years, simultaneously rocked the country. Following the crises, financial and political instabilities fed into each other and eroded the citizens' trust in their economic and political systems.

In the succeeding decades, symptoms that were similar to those appearing in Italy – economic stagnation, social fragmentation, political polarization and democratic vulnerability – emerged in several other advanced societies. What happened to Italy after the 1990s is revealing of the quality of public life in western democracies and around the world. However, understanding Italy's recent economic parabola requires an investigation of some of the country's secular characteristics.

Even after its unification in the nineteenth century, Italy remained a divided country. Geographical, cultural and economic differences have run deep through Italy's society, typically between the country's North and South. Mending those differences required a difficult political exercise, distributing the costs and benefits among citizens. When resources were scarcer, or social cohesion was under pressure, public indebtment became the government's favorite tool for keeping the country together.

However, at the beginning of the 1990s, the level of Italy's public debt became a source of financial instability, augmenting the unprecedented shakiness of the political system at the time. According to our findings, political and financial precarity concurred in causing a sharp decline in investment and technology. In 1996, after surpassing America's level, Italy's productivity started losing pace with respect to the other advanced economies.

In the following decades, Italy's economy slowed down until it stopped growing completely, and even declined in absolute terms. The predicaments of the last few decades have forced one part of the economy to become increasingly resilient and another part increasingly weak. Those divides are reminiscent of the century-old rooted distance between individual economic vitalism and public authorities and they explain why the country is both reactive and difficult to govern.

By studying the Italian malaise over time, this book often mixes economic and political interpretations. This is slippery terrain, especially when analyses span across centuries.

We would like to thank Manuela Mischitelli, who helped us verify the consistency of the interpretations in the data, and our colleagues at LUISS University for contributing with ideas and comments. Special thanks go to Giuseppe Laterza, who allowed us to use here some of the reflections from our earlier book, *La Strada Smarrita* (Laterza 2020).

1 | *Italy's Parabola, 1861–2022*

There were years in Italy's history when genius and ambition seemed to know no limit. In 1492 Christopher Columbus, a navigator from Genoa, discovered a new continent as he tried to reach India by sailing west. Three years later, between 1495 and 1496, Leonardo da Vinci started painting the Last Supper in Milan. Michelangelo returned to his native Florence and paid his first visit to Rome, where he would create eternal masterpieces. In Venice, the equestrian statue of condottiero Bartolomeo Colleoni was erected as a sign of the Republic's wealth and power. At that time, Venice, Florence and Milan were the wealthiest areas in Europe, and probably the world. According to some estimates, Italians were on average better off by about 30 percent than the rest of Western Europeans. Northern Italy was possibly almost twice as rich as the average region in France, Spain or England.

Being used to dominating seas and trade, in 1495 the Venetians understood that, after Columbus's "discovery" of America, the Mediterranean Sea was bound to lose its centrality. Rumors spread among the Venetian merchants about Portuguese ships preparing to circumnavigate Africa before the end of the century. The Council of Ten, the collegium presiding over government decisions of the Venetian Republic, could not dither. The representatives of the patrician families were summoned to the Palazzo Ducale, which was still under reconstruction after the disastrous fire of 1483. Whoever visits Venice today knows exactly the huge palace standing next to St. Mark's Basilica overlooking the lagoon and decorated with Gothic arches and colonnades. Even today, the Council's strategy seems so daring as to challenge our understanding of those ages: The collegium advanced a proposal to introduce a tax in the following years to finance the digging of a canal between the African and the Asian continents. It is the same canal that would be built centuries later and would become known as the Suez Canal.

In 1495, Venetian Doge Agostino Barbarigo led a coalition that chased the French forces out of Italy. It was time for Venice to defend its role in global trade. Venetian engineers were sent to Egypt to study the feasibility of the new canal and came back with a favorable opinion: The available technology was sufficient for carrying out the project, that is, connecting a string of local lakes and linking the Mediterranean to the Red Sea. The canal would have shortened the routes to India and China dramatically, more than compensated for Venice's inability to trade with the New World, connected the Middle East to the world's most developed economies, contained the role of the Ottomans, and most importantly, maintained Venice at the center of the world.

The final project was presented on May 4, 1504. Unfortunately for Venice, Egyptian Sultan Qaansuuh al-Gawri opposed the project and on June 11, 1504, the Council of Ten symbolically drew a black cross on the engineers' map (Pedani 2012). The project had to wait 355 years, till the middle of the nineteenth century, to become reality.

To consolidate its power and wealth, Venice had to look back at Italy's mainland. It was Pope Julius II this time to see Venice's expansion as a threat to the secular powers of the Roman Church in Central and Southern Italy. He excommunicated the Venetian Republic and called for foreign military powers to contain it. Soon Italy became a playground for foreign powers. In 1530 Holy Roman Emperor Charles V subjugated the Tuscan republics, the Kingdom of Naples and the Duchy of Milan. The two major Italian seafaring powers, Venice and Genoa, fighting each other in the Mediterranean, were unable to adapt their institutions and technology and seize the opportunities offered to them by the trans-oceanic challenge. They were small and geography, it was said, was against them; also, in the bellicose environment, their defensive mentality prevented them from absorbing new ideas, and techniques and from embracing new challenges. According to various scholars, including Carlo Maria Cipolla (2013), the cultural and institutional resistance to change slowly produced an economic decline.[1] Presumably, foreign domination eroded Italy's social fabric and the relevance of cultural life, as reveals the common dictum "France or Spain, as long as we eat grain,"[2] presciently pronounced by Machiavelli's friend Francesco Guicciardini. The desolating "Spanish" domination of Italy was only one reason for the long period of fragmentation, internal conflicts and foreign invasions that made the states of the Italian peninsula, for many centuries probably the wealthiest in the world, one of Western Europe's poorest.

Starting from the late sixteenth century, the economy of the Italian states declined in relative terms. According to some estimates, in the seventeenth century, the decline turned into an absolute loss of income (Malanima 2003, Broadberry 2016). Economic primacy in Europe passed to the United Provinces of the Netherlands, which had their own "golden age" until the mid-eighteenth century when that primacy passed to the British Isles, which maintained it until WWI. Already in the late nineteenth century, per capita income in the United States, the lands discovered by Columbus, exceeded that of the United Kingdom (Kindleberger 1996).

In the second half of the eighteenth century and the first two decades of the nineteenth century, Italy's per capita income did not grow and probably shrank. At the end of the Napoleonic Wars, real wages were lower than they had been around 1700, one of every four newborns died in his or her first months, and even the height of the average Italian male noticeably shrank from 167 cm in the mid-eighteenth century to 164 cm at the beginning of the nineteenth. There was some progress but, at the time of unification in 1861, Italy's economic misery had not changed much for the better.

Declines can last for a long time, centuries in this case, before they reverse course. The renewed attention to the Italian economy focuses on the second decline that occurred in the first decades of the twenty-first century, one, however, caused by factors that bore resemblance to those that caused the first: global competition, political uncertainty and economic regression. After the protracted and impetuous growth between the end of the nineteenth century and the end of the twentieth, Italy's economy, surprisingly, became poorer again, first in relative terms and, after the Great Recession of 2008–2013, even in absolute terms. There is no other instance of an advanced industrial economy experiencing a similar decline, and no other democratic nation has had to cope with the impoverishment of its new generations. As scholars debate the possible decline of the West and of western democracies, Italy seems to have preceded the trend, testing the resilience of its liberal democracy.

Italy has often anticipated social and political phenomena that later appeared in other countries: the decline of liberalism and the emergence of fascism; geographical polarization; mistrust in public institutions; recourse to public debt; secular stagnation; populism. Italy, however, has also been a laboratory in the constant attempt to amend these phenomena: the antifascist resistance; massive inter-regional aid; widespread entrepreneurship; uninterrupted reforms of the political system; the accumulation of private (and public) savings; the judiciary fight against the Mafia or corruption; the support for European sovereignty and supranational cooperation; and the correction of populist choices through non-partisan governments. Ironically, if Austrian philosopher Karl Popper was right in defining democracy not as the way to elect the best of governments, but as the way to take down the bad ones, by changing sixty-seven governments between WWII and 2022, Italy's democratic credentials must be at the forefront.

The reasons why Italy tends to anticipate the phenomena associated with a fragile democracy are conventionally ascribed to the fact that, since its foundation, the Kingdom of Italy's political–institutional order has been perceived as weak, particularly in comparison with the neighboring foreign powers. In the early nineteenth century, while Friedrich Hegel was chanting the quintessential link between Spirit and Power, more humbly, Alessandro Manzoni, the author of the novel *The Betrothed*, which is compulsory reading for all young Italian students, observed how the weakness of the state was "a more famous than understood trait of homeland history." This book sheds light on the interaction between economic choices and the peculiar relationship that runs between Italians and their state.

Italy's recent decline has elicited standard narratives reconnecting its recent impoverishment with the experience of the known past. Political instability and foreign domination between the seventeenth and the nineteenth centuries, at a time when beyond Italy's borders the great nation-states were being strengthened, have long been the preferred explanations of Italy's economic decline. In the following pages, we will trace the fault lines running through Italian history that may resonate with contemporary political–economic analysis in other countries. We identify several divisions in Italy's society that have been overcome by using state finance while that was possible. Rather than changing its incentives for the population, the government chose public debt to preserve the status quo, which has emerged as a political preference or necessity in a fragmented and polarized country. The consequence has been the crystallization of structural problems.

It is our tenet that domestic divergences, political inefficiency, public debt, financial instability and lower quality in investment have represented the links of the same causality chain. Among the internal divisions, the regional divergence between North and South was the most persistent, often coinciding with different levels of education and technological advancement. Other differences have played a major role in individual historical periods: for instance, popular estrangement from the process of constitution of the unified state; the drastic ideological polarization after WWII; the winners-vs.-losers of several monetary shocks; or an exacerbated level of popular suspicion of seemingly corrupt elites. Moreover, weak statehood and structural cleavages were mutually reinforcing.

However, one crucial argument in our reconstruction of Italy's economic evolution is that factors of political weakness have often coexisted with the strength of the economy. The apparent distance of citizens from public life runs parallel to the vibrancy of local communities and social structures and the worldliness of a part of the country's elite, which emerged through non-political "technocratic" government formations. Throughout its history Italy has often engaged non-political personnel in the highest public offices: Orlando, Nitti, De Stefani, Rocco, Beneduce, Menichella, Badoglio, Einaudi, Amato, Ciampi, Monti and Draghi, among others. Openness to the external world was a constant necessity for an economy depending on foreign provisions for raw materials or financial capital: non-partisan leadership often went hand in hand with the voluntary acceptance of external economic constraints or, as erstwhile Bank of Italy governor Guido Carli theorized, spontaneous limitations of national sovereignty and discretional policies, which, in turn, may have contributed to "horizontal legitimacy," that is, strengthening the country's credibility in its interaction with the international community.[3]

Italians' ambivalence toward the state was probably sedimented by centuries of foreign domination. Between the seventeenth and nineteenth centuries, the fatalism of subjection, liable to vary over time according to those who exercise it, generated passivity and extraneousness from public life, long dominated by local princes and foreign lords engaged in opportunistic behavior and obscure games of alliances and betrayals. In the conventional sociological interpretation, the individual had little other option but to leverage the relationship of personal devotion, a patron/client relationship, or to break rules and even laws.

Once the possibility of engaging in public affairs had been banned, all that remained was to devote oneself to private trade.

We see a dialectic tension between Italians' economic commitment and their political disenchantment. Throughout Italy's history, the two planes, political and economic, moved at different speeds. But in the 1990s a profound crisis in the state coincided with economic decline. Financial and political instabilities concurred to hamper Italy's development exactly in the years when new and groundbreaking global technological paradigms required investment in the future. A whole chapter is devoted to the multiple crises of the early 1990s, as we see them being the root of the subsequent economic decline.

We will argue that political uncertainty spiked in 1992, affecting Italy's outsized public debt and financial system, resulting in growing interest rate differentials with other European economies. Our findings indicate that the divarication of Italy's financial conditions had a major impact on the quantity and quality of investments. For these reasons, Italy partly missed the train of the technological revolution of the 1990s. Since then, Italy's productivity has diminished, bringing the economy into a vicious circle of lower growth, higher debt and increasing political instability.

In terms of the decline, institutional, political and economic factors have frequently interacted with each other. In a system of global competition, public powers are not irrelevant, and a vibrant economy is not self-sufficient. A democratic state and an open economy rest on a government's ability to respond to issues coming from both the domestic society and the external world. In short, the evolution of Italy's economy in the twenty-first century is also an anticipatory example of democracy's complex adjustment to globalization.

Considering the precarity perceived in many other democracies, under the pressure of globalized markets, internal divergences, political polarization, high public debts or autocratic temptations, Italy's experience tells a revealing story of the West resisting its own decline.

At the time of Italy's political unification, in March 1861, the shining lights of the Renaissance were long gone. The ages when Venice and Florence were leading European civilization had faded into poverty and backwardness. For centuries, regional divisions and hostilities among local autocrats or feudal elites, steered also by foreign domination, had eroded Italy's physical wealth and human prosperity (Table1.1).

Table 1.1 *GDP per person 1500–1870 (US dollars at 1990 purchasing power)*

Year	Italy	UK	France	Germany	Japan	12 Western European countries	Italy's GDP per capita in % of Western Europe
1500	1100	714	727	676	500	796	138
1820	1117	1706	1230	1058	669	1270	89
1870	1499	3191	1876	1821	737	2086	72

Source: Maddison (2010)[4]

In 1861, despite some progress made since the 1820s, the average gross domestic product (GDP) per inhabitant, that is, the present-day quantity of goods and services produced on average for one year by each citizen, did not exceed 70 percent of Western Europe's average and was less than 50 percent of the United Kingdom's, the most economically advanced country of the era. To get an idea of the poverty plaguing Italy at the time, one may consider that the average annual income of an Italian around 1870 was about 2,050 present-day euros, that is, 170 euros per month, an income not higher than that of most of today's sub-Saharan countries. Moreover, given the extremely uneven income distribution, the living standard of most inhabitants of the Italian peninsula was not far from, and sometimes below, mere subsistence: forty-four percent of the population had to live on less than 83 euros per month, which is below the threshold of absolute poverty (Vecchi 2017: 359).

Italians' average lifespan did not reach thirty years (Vecchi 2017: 90), while in France and Sweden it was forty-five. This was due mainly, but not only, to the second highest infant mortality rate in Europe, after the German one (Vecchi 2017: 108): Over a quarter of newborns did not reach their first birthday. Even in today's poorest countries, the average lifespan is considerably longer. In what was the cradle of the Renaissance and humanism, education was the privilege of a few. In 1861, only 26 percent of Italians over the age of fifteen could read and write. In 1870, Italians on average had less than one year of formal education, compared to four years for British citizens and six years for Americans (Vecchi 2017: 176). The new kingdom, therefore, was born poor and was under the burden of significant inequalities both in income and wealth.

The composition of employment in Italy was also typical of a backward economy, with 63 percent of the labor force employed, often underemployed, in agriculture. The industrial sector accounted for only about 17 percent of total employment (Baffigi 2013). Manufacturing activities took place mostly in small enterprises and workshops, normally employing all the members of a family[5] and producing little more than the common goods of daily life: food, apparel and furniture. In the mid-nineteenth century, one-third of the Italian manufacturers produced food, another third furniture and construction, and one-fifth apparel. The silk products supplied by the small firms in the Alpine regions, from Piedmont to Friuli, formed the basis of the local productive bourgeoisie and capital accumulation. Italy's exports covered most of the European demand for sophisticated textiles. The industry was beginning to produce substantial revenues to pay for the raw materials with which the country was poorly endowed. Infrastructure was also considerably less developed than in the advanced countries of Northwestern Europe. In 1861, the Italian peninsula had only 2,404 kilometers of railway, mostly located in the North, while Great Britain had 14,603 and the area of the future German Reich 11,603.

At the end of 1858, just before the beginning of the Second Italian War of Independence,[6] which led to the birth of the Kingdom of Italy, the Italian peninsula was divided into eight states (Fig. 1.1).

More than fifteen centuries of political disunion, often marked by fierce fighting among cities and states, had resulted in deeply rooted cultural, institutional–political and economic differences across the various parts of the peninsula. Tullio De Mauro (1963), a leading glottologist, estimated that, around the time of the proclamation of the new unified kingdom, only 2.5 percent of its citizens could shed their local dialect and communicate in Italian.[7] French was the working language in the Turin Parliament, the only elected legislative body on the peninsula.

Given that the "Southern question," or, generally speaking, the economic, social and cultural gap between the various areas of the country, is to this day the most salient feature of Italian society, it is worth considering these gaps at the beginning of our story. In fact, the issue of the "initial conditions," that is, the real economic backwardness of the Southern regions at the time of unification, still looms large in the debate on regional disparities today. Since the beginning of the century, a considerable amount of quantitative research has improved our knowledge of the main economic aggregates by region and province. A consensus seems to emerge pointing to smaller income gaps around the time of unification than existed in later years. Daniele and Malanima (2007) plausibly argue that, with average income levels close to subsistence, regional disparities could not have been large. In fact, Felice (2007) puts Southern GDP per capita in 1871 to 10 percent below the national average, with a wide within-South variance. Iuzzolino et al. (2013) estimate manufacturing output per capita to have been 30 percent lower in the South relative to the Northwest, but only 10 percent below the national average. Fenoaltea (2007) identifies

Figure 1.1 Map: The Italian peninsula before unification (1848)
Source: Toniolo, 2013

an East–West gap in addition to the traditional North–South rift. In
fact, geographical analysis at a more disaggregate level than the
regional one shows that economic and social divisions ran deep even
within relatively limited areas.

Income and production data, however, are not entirely consistent
with the well-being indicators that are normally significantly correlated
with GDP per capita. In 1861, the height of the military recruits, quite

a good comprehensive indicator of well-being, was 163.7 centimeters in the Northwest as against 160.9 in the South (Vecchi 2011: 57). The educational gap was even wider: Only 15 percent of the population over fifteen years of age could read and write in the South versus 48 percent in the Northwest. Likewise, Vecchi and Toniolo (2007) found a higher incidence of child labor in the South than in the Central and Northern regions.

In 2007, about a century and a half after Italy's political unification, the quantity of goods and services (GDP) available on average to each Italian was roughly twelve times greater than in 1861. The average lifespan (life expectancy at birth) was about eighty-two years, higher than in any other European country and the second highest in the world, after Japan. Only 27 out of 10,000 children did not reach the first year of age, a much lower number than in the United States. Income distribution was much more egalitarian than at the time of the unification; five percent of the population lived in absolute poverty, a number that is still too high for a G7 country but far from the 40 percent that characterized the Italian peninsula around 1861. Illiteracy had (almost) been completely eradicated, even if – as we will see – the quantity and quality of education did not live up to that of other countries with a similar income per capita and was still inadequate to allow Italy to take full advantage of the new technologies. All Italian regions had participated in this extraordinary process of economic growth and collective well-being, although not uniformly. The poorer areas did not reduce the income gap between themselves and the most prosperous ones, something that was already evident in the early twentieth century.

The revolutionary process that forever changed the living conditions of Italians was common to that of the many countries that took the path of "Modern Economic Growth" (MEG) between the nineteenth and twentieth centuries. Nobel laureate Simon Kuznets (1966) characterized MEG as the "epochal revolution," by far the most important in the whole history of humanity, not only because it relieved the vast majority of the world's population from the poverty of the previous millennia, but also because it allowed this majority to realize dreams that seemed unrealistic until the mid-nineteenth century: not only freedom from hunger but longer and healthier life, shorter and less tiring working schedules, education, geographical and even social mobility – the latter being almost unimaginable for millennia. If Italy's MEG is not an exception within the "club" of countries that undertook the process sometime in the nineteenth century, her early participation in the "club" was not discounted at the time of unification by both Italian and foreign observers. In the early twentieth century, neither British Prime Minister Arthur Balfour, nor Giovanni Giolitti, his Italian counterpart, would have bet a bottle of claret on Italy's GDP per capita being higher than Britain's eighty years afterward.

Economists and economic historians expect initially lower-income countries to "converge" (catch-up) with the more developed ones. There are good reasons for such expectations: Technologies are cheaper to copy than to develop, affluent foreign markets are good outlets for cheap (labor-intensive) products of poorer countries and the evidence of MEG benefits provides social and political motivation to follow the same route. Nonetheless, history shows that the eventuality of poorer countries catching up with richer ones is far from being a universal phenomenon. In fact, for most of the past two centuries, it was the exception rather than the rule. Catching up (or convergence, in economic jargon) requires "social capability for growth" to sustain apt policies over the long run (Abramovitz 1986). Such capability is built on a mix of cultural, social and institutional factors. They are not endowed by nature but need to be created and maintained. Our history will focus on how and when Italy generated and sustained growth-enhancing conditions. For roughly a century (from the mid-1890s to the mid-1990s) such conditions were maintained, although with different degrees of success at different times. This long catching-up epoch in Italy's economic history is encapsulated between two periods of "falling behind" the more advanced countries of the time, each period lasting about thirty years. Italy's economic history is therefore interesting for studying the reasons for both how a poor country started and sustained its MEG and how it lost a part of its "social capability for growth." The latter question, as we will see, is particularly intriguing for the thirty-odd years following the early 1990s.

Before describing and analyzing the various phases of Italy's economic history since the unification, it may be useful to examine the overall quantitative picture. Between 1870, the first year for which internationally comparable data exist, and 2007, Italy's real GDP per capita grew at an annual rate of about 1.9 percent, slightly higher than the average of the other Western European countries and roughly equal to the growth rate of the United States. As mentioned above,

Table 1.2 *GDP and well-being indicators 1861–2007*

	1861	2007
GDP per capita (euros at 2007 prices)	2,190	26,457
Life expectancy at birth (years)	30	82
First-year death rate (per 1000)	289	4.5
Income distribution (Gini coefficient)	0.50	0.33
People in absolute poverty (% of resident population)	40	5
Literacy rate (% of resident population)	22	98

Source: Toniolo (2013:4)

however, this overall picture is the result of a long period of "convergence" framed between two periods of "divergence." Table 1.2 provides a rough idea of the orders of magnitude of both phenomena. Using the United Kingdom (the pioneer in MEG) as a benchmark, Italy's GDP per capita lost considerable ground during the first thirty years after its political unification. Only at the end of the nineteenth century, after overcoming a serious economic, political and social crisis, did the economy of the new kingdom accelerate the pace of its development. We will see the non-linear dynamic of the long convergence that brought Italy's income per capita, which in 1896 was about 60 percent of that of Germany and France, to be roughly equal to that of these two countries at the end of the twentieth century (Table 1.3). Even more impressive was the "catching up" with the United Kingdom, which at the end of the nineteenth century enjoyed a per capita income of about two and a half times the Italian one. A century later, Italy's GDP per capita was equal to, and by some measures even higher than, that of the "first industrial nation."

Between 1896 and 1995, the convergence of labor productivity was even more evident than it was for GDP per capita. By the mid-1990s production per hour by an Italian worker was very close to that of his or her American peer (Fig. 3.1). We will see in Chapter 3 the main features of this long convergence process, detailing the moments when it was more or less rapid, its weaknesses alongside its strengths.

As the result of previous growth, in 1995 Italy's economic problems were no longer those typical of a relatively backward country. In most respects, Italy was part of the club of advanced countries, albeit with more relevant structural problems than other economies. From that

Table 1.3 *Italy's GDP per capita as percentage of GDP per capita in four developed countries (US dollars at 1990 purchasing power)*

Year	USA	Germany	France	United Kingdom
1871	61	91	82	50
1896	46	59	61	38
1913	46	70	70	52
1938	54	66	74	53
1973	64	89	83	90
1995	70	89	94	98
2007	62	96	88	85
2016	53	77	78	72

Sources: from 1861 to 1973: Maddison 2010, Historical Statistics of the World Economy, 0–2008, OECD, Paris (2010); from 1995 to 2016, The Conference Board (www.conference-board.org/data/).

moment on, it was a question of keeping up with the others. To do so, Italy could no longer count on the "advantages of backwardness" and on the business and economic policy strategies associated with them. A change of pace, both in the private and the public sector, was necessary. However, it did not take place, or at least there was not enough of it. The economy stalled. By 2007, the gap with the more advanced countries had returned to the levels of the 1970s. Convergence had given way to divergence. In the decades before 2020, Italy's growth tapered off and eventually came to a halt. In living memory, no other advanced economy in a democratic country has ever experienced a similar ebb of its economic dynamism.

According to Acemoglu and Robinson (2012),[8] inclusive institutions, democratic and pluralistic states, guarantee the rule of law and promote economic prosperity by appreciating and giving free rein to talents and creative ideas. They provide what economists call an incentive structure for individuals, a framework that acknowledges and rewards individual initiative. On the contrary, extractive institutions, those that permit the ruling elite to exploit the majority of the population, deter economic growth. Italy's post-1995 decline, which we will try to describe, is of a different kind. It resembles a democratic country that lost itself after vibrant century-long economic development. After achieving economic convergence with the most advanced societies, when democratic participation was strongest and a robust self-critical analysis was underway, Italy's economic growth slowed dramatically, and eventually stopped altogether. At that juncture, political life lost credibility and uncertainty clouded the future of a large majority of Italians.

Italy's institutional problems were not those of a backward society. In the 1990s Italy was a fully accomplished democracy, with voting participation of almost 90 percent. Its level of income was as high as in Britain, Germany or France. Italy's institutional problems were of a different kind, and they may serve as a lesson for other advanced democracies. The cause of Italy's prolonged economic stagnation was an unusual alchemic combination of multiple explosive crises that might represent a cautionary tale for other advanced societies complacent about their welfare and their democratic development. The mysterious "Italian disease" started to take root at the peak of Italy's economic miracle less than twenty years after WWII, long before the onset of the economic decline of the 1990s. Since then, we have seen similar symptoms – geographic divergences, growing debts, populist policies, political instability, degradation of public discourse and sentiments of mistrust in the civic community – spread all over the western world at an alarming and accelerating pace. Italy's history shows that, at some stage, a slowly developing and long ignored disease reaches a tipping point.

2 | *Slow Economic Unification, 1861–1896*

2.1 Political Unification as an Opportunity for Growth

On June 4, 1859, the allied armies of France and Piedmont crossed the river Ticino, at the border between the (Piedmont) Kingdom of Sardinia and Austrian Lombardy, to crush Vienna's army near the town of Magenta. Five days later, French Emperor Napoleon III and Sardinian King Vittorio Emanuele II entered Milan. Momentous events followed in rapid sequence, leading, in less than two years, to the unification of the states of the peninsula into the newly created Kingdom of Italy.

Austria ceded Lombardy to Vittorio Emanuele II, the only constitutional monarch in Italy, but kept Veneto, roughly corresponding to the territory of the erstwhile Republic of Venice. France, and to a lesser extent Great Britain, wanted to create a large independent state in Northern Italy, although without radically upsetting the existing European order. History, however, took a different path. Popular uprisings in the states of Parma, Modena and Tuscany forced the local rulers to leave. Hastily organized plebiscites sanctioned their annexation to the Kingdom of Sardinia. On May 5, 1860, Garibaldi's thousand soldiers, the legendary "red shirts," sailed from Quarto, a Ligurian harbor, and landed in the Sicilian town of Marsala under the benevolent eye of two Royal Navy frigates. The "Thousand" swiftly conquered the island, crossed the Strait of Messina and triumphantly entered Naples on September 7, 1860. The political unification of the Italian peninsula was complete, except for Veneto and a much-curtailed Papal State. On March 17, 1861, Vittorio Emanuele II was proclaimed King of Italy. The war of 1866, in which the newly created Italian state allied with Prussia against Austria, added Venice and its surrounding region to the Kingdom of Italy. Rome was annexed in 1870, after the fall of Napoleon III, hitherto the guarantor of the Pope's independence.

The process leading to the creation of a single independent state is known as the Risorgimento[1] ("the revival"). Economic concerns were not the main ideological and political drivers of the unification's architects. Their main aim was to replace foreign rule with a single Italian constitutional democracy; some of them even advocated a republican regime. They hoped that freedom from foreign dominance and the establishment of liberal institutions would also revive the economy (Ciocca 2007: 70–72). Since the 1840s, the leaders of the Risorgimento, such as Vincenzo Gioberti, Cesare Balbo, and Massimo D'Azeglio, had advanced a political platform that contained references to the economic question,[2] in particular concerning trade liberalization. A Customs League between the Italian states proposed by Pope Pio IX in 1847, following the model of the German *Zollverein*, received widespread approval across the various Italian states. The project, however, was destroyed by the revolutions of 1848–1849; therefore, contrary to the German case, the political unification of Italy was not preceded by a customs union. Economic motivation was, however, present in the Kingdom of Sardinia – sometimes dubbed Italy's "little Prussia" for its driving role in the unification – under Camillo Benso di Cavour's leadership. Believing that the state's role in promoting economic development consisted largely in creating adequate social overhead capital (infrastructures), Cavour promoted the excavation of canals, the extension of the rail network and the improvement of Genoa's harbor. A compulsory elementary education Act was passed by Turin's Parliament. In 1855 a new tariff law, inspired by ideas of free trade, drastically reduced import duties.

The Kingdom of Italy was born at a time when the first era of globalization was gaining full steam. Falling transportation costs and the spread of free trade policies, following the repeal of the British Corn Laws, produced a gradual reduction of European import duties throughout the 1850s (Findlay and O'Rourke 2007: 396). In 1860, France and the United Kingdom signed the so-called Cobden Chevalier Treaty, which, by incorporating the "most favored nation clause," produced additional incentives for the reduction of tariff barriers by European countries. Throughout Western Europe GDP growth accelerated. Germany, in particular, was rapidly catching up with the United Kingdom, the cradle of industrial development. Italy's political unification, therefore, took place at a time when international economic conditions were favorable also to an economic Risorgimento, after the completion of the political one. The international economic environment was advantageous for growth acceleration by a latecomer to industrial development, one that could exploit the technology transfers from more advanced nations, as well as foreign capital inflows, labor mobility and the export of agricultural and labor-intensive manufactured goods. For about three decades after unification, however, the new kingdom did not take advantage of such favorable opportunities. Italy's GDP growth only slightly exceeded the 1850–1860 pace, too slowly for the new country to catch up with Europe's more advanced Northwest and meet the expectations of those Italian citizens who had seen the end of foreign autocratic rule as a prerequisite for increased prosperity.

Political unification resulted in the creation of probably the world's eighth-largest economy. Italians were relatively poor, but they were numerous: the 1871 census counted about 26 million citizens. By comparison, the United Kingdom's population was 30 million and the most populous pre-unification state, the Kingdom of the Two Sicilies, only counted 9 million subjects. Demography was a relevant geopolitical factor. Unification created "the least of the great powers" (Bosworth 1979) or, as someone later maliciously said, just "the first of the small powers." Whatever the case, political unification potentially entailed two growth-enhancing factors: economic policy autonomy and a large single market. The pre-unification states had limited economic policy autonomy due to their small size and direct or indirect foreign domination. This was particularly true for their monetary regimes, government debt and tariff policies. Unification allowed the new national government to enjoy wider maneuvering room in monetary policy (e.g., the convertibility regime of banknotes), easier and cheaper access to foreign markets for government borrowing and adequate import duty structures. At least in principle, monetary, fiscal and trade policies could be designed to favor economic development. The most important potential economic benefit of unification was, however, the creation of a single market of 26 million people. The advantages of a larger national market had not escaped the attention of the Risorgimento's leaders. In the 1840s, Vincenzo Gioberti advocated a federation of independent states, bound together by a customs union (Gioberti 1845), along the lines of the German *Zollverein*. Unfortunately, nothing came of it. Had Italy followed Germany in creating a single market before political unification, the dawn of the Kingdom of Italy would have taken place in a stronger economic environment, leveraging on the comparative advantages of the multi-farious resource endowments of the Italian regions. On the contrary, before 1861, the peninsula was made up of several small, closed economies. The degree of openness (i.e., the ratio of imports and exports to the gross domestic product) had been around 40 percent in the Kingdom of Sardinia (Graziani 1960), but only 20 percent in the Austrian Kingdom of Lombardy-Venetia, in the Emilian Duchies and the Grand Duchy of Tuscany. The Papal States and the Bourbon Kingdom of Naples, with a 10 percent degree of openness, were essentially closed economies. Furthermore, the modest external trade of the South was directed almost entirely outside the Italian peninsula, accounting for only 13 percent of the Kingdom of Naples' international trade (Zamagni 2007: 42–43). Another important expected effect of market unification was what economists call "trade diversion," the substitution of old trade partners with new ones. Until 1860, the Austrian Kingdom of Lombardy-Venetia was part of the Austrian Empire's customs union. After unification, while customs disappeared with the rest of Italy, trade barriers were set up with the Central European territories of the Austrian Empire, with the consequent "diversion" of traffic. For some of the former Italian subjects of the Austrian Empire this was not good news (any diversion involves significant adjustment costs), but traders and producers from the rest of Italy benefited from the new situation.

Other potential economic benefits of unification were expected from the end of foreign domination and the replacement of absolutist monarchies with constitutional governments. The economy was likely to benefit from what we today refer to as "the rule of law" and better "human capital": checks and balances between the executive, legislative and judicial powers; greater certainty of habeas corpus; new civil and commercial codes; the diffusion of compulsory primary education; and increased freedom to undertake economic activities. Other expected benefits would come from the reduction in transaction costs due to the unification of currency, weights and measures, stock exchanges, bank regulations and taxation systems.

2.2 Disappointing Growth

Given the *ex ante* potential benefits of the political unification, the *ex post* economic performance of the new kingdom fell short of

expectations. Between 1861 and 1896, Italy's GDP per capita grew at
an average annual rate of about 0.6 percent, an acceleration from the
previous decade but hardly enough to catch up with the richer Western
European countries, which on average were growing more than twice
as fast as Italy. The gap between the most advanced economies and
Italy widened. During the thirty-odd years following political unification, the centuries-long relative economic decline continued, albeit at a
slower pace.

What were the reasons for the apparently disappointing
performance of unified Italy over the first three decades of its existence?
A short general answer is that political unification could not be
expected to result in overnight economic unification. If it took a short
period to obtain the former, the latter had to overcome centuries of
political, institutional and cultural fragmentation.

The new Italian state was made up of regions that had their own
legal traditions, economic institutions, currencies, business practices
and laws. More important, though difficult to quantify, were the
cultural and linguistic differences. Italy was born with a low level of
social capital. Italians did not trust each other and did not trust their
governments. Over the following decades, mistrust was reduced but
never overcome; and, as we shall see, it has remained a constant feature
of Italian society, with a pervasive impact on the economy.

2.3 Cultural and Political Flaws of Unification

Among the various reasons for the citizens' mistrust of the state was
the so-called Catholic question. It had emerged in the Risorgimento
and divided the new country for about half a century after unification.
The liberal political ideology inspiring the "fathers of the homeland"
was – or was seen to be – inconsistent with traditional Catholic beliefs.
This was surely a problem with the majority of the population, but not
an insurmountable one. Influential people like poet and novelist
Alessandro Manzoni were known as "liberal Catholics." Piedmont's
Prime Minister Cavour, the unification's political mastermind, personally not a devout Catholic, was perfectly aware that Catholicism was
deeply rooted in Italian culture and society; so much so that, shortly
before his untimely death in 1861, in a speech to the Senate he presciently advocated an agreement between the state and the Church, even
though he knew that, once the agreement was reached, "the

proponents of the Church, that I here call the Catholic Party, would gain the majority of parliamentary seats." In that case, he added, "I am already resigned to end my career on the opposition's benches."[3] The conquest of Rome in 1870 – with the confiscation of the Church's land and properties and with the Italian king occupying the Quirinal Palace, the Pope's residence – made an agreement between the Church and the state impossible for a long period. In 1874, Pope Pius IX, considering himself a prisoner of the Italian state in the Vatican, used the Latin formula *non expedit* (it is not appropriate) to warn Catholics not to seek office or vote in Italian elections. Only in 1905 did Pio X, while not formally revoking the order, allow Catholics to participate in public life when circumstances seemed to be appropriate. The *non expedit* measure was not fully abolished until 1919 when Pope Benedict XV allowed Catholics to join the Popular Party, led by Luigi Sturzo, a priest. For almost half a century, Catholic citizens, the majority in the country, had been marginalized from the establishment of the new economic, political and social institutions.

From a cultural perspective, the proclamation of the Kingdom of Italy did not unite the country. The construction of a nation by a bourgeois elite in a country of peasants, at the hands of a convent of Freemasons in a nation of Catholics, gave new support to anti-political sentiments along with a stigma of illegitimacy on the unitary state. New institutions were alien to, and often disliked by, the masses, both Catholic and socialist, and to entire territories, primarily the South, or "Affrica," as Cavour's lieutenant in Naples, Carlo Farini, contemptuously misspelled it. The elite leading the political process was mainly composed of landowners or entrepreneurs who admired the economic development underway in France and the United Kingdom. Many of them had no idea of, nor interest in, the situation in the South. The delay and the conflicting way in which Italy created a unitary state are probably not the last of the reasons for the lack of trust that the political establishment has suffered ever since, and for the scarce consideration reserved for public office. The political class was described by Catholic publicists as being reduced to "an army of 'fast-handed' bankers, or conjurers of public and private fortunes, or thaumaturges of the stamped paper" (Chiarini 2021). It was a class intent only on "hunting for power." Catholic intellectuals introduced the distinction between *paese legale* (legal country) and *paese reale* (real country) and insisted on the illegitimacy of power usurped by a few at the expense of the many. The detachment between the *paese legale* and the *paese reale* remained vivid as women were excluded from voting until 1945, while universal male suffrage was not introduced until 1912. Since the first years of Italy's unification, literature desecrating the democratic function of the new Parliament was already flourishing. In popular books and media, members of parliament were described as schemers, all absorbed by their private interests and often trespassing into the territory of direct personal business.

Besides the clerical opposition expressed in the Pope's *non expedit*, the socialist movement also took an anti-establishment stance in defense of the "excluded people." Political scientists note that the Marxist movement, lacking a theory of the state at least until the beginning of the twentieth century, mused about the suppression of political ordainment and the end of politics. Parliamentary activity was sometimes delegitimized as a means of conflict resolution, as it was perceived to be aimed at the maintenance of incumbent powers against the people. Even within the bourgeoisie an anti-political elite existed with a generation of patriots opposed to the Ancien Régime and to the Church, which they viewed as imbued with Austrian nostalgia. The emphasis placed by the bourgeois elite on the enhancement of industriousness and resourcefulness, on the dissemination of education and on the superiority of merit over privilege ended up shaping a civic ethos that was tinged with mistrust toward the state.

The Italian state only slowly developed according to the "fiscal-military state" model, defined by George Washington as "the power of making war, peace, and treaties, that of levying money and regulating commerce, and the correspondent executive and judicial authorities,"[4] in which there is a clear link between the legislative power, the public administration and a professional body of public officials. In 1878, after meeting with Francesco Crispi, who had been sent to Berlin by the King of Italy to offer a military alliance against France, German Reichskanzler Otto von Bismarck observed: "I could count on a state and an army, he could count on neither."[5] From its inception, the Italian Kingdom was seen by some Italians as an artificial construct, one that lacked the complete process of nation and state building. Liberal intellectual Piero Gobetti observed that Italy was a state not believed by its people, who had not shed their blood to create it. A similar assessment was expressed by communist thinker Antonio Gramsci, who deemed that the popular masses had remained estranged from the building of the state. Many in the South saw the political-administrative unification as a "royal conquest" by the Kingdom of Sardinia, a construction imposed by the North through inefficient Southern administrative personnel. The perception of Sardinian institutional continuity was made evident by the king maintaining his Savoyard name, Vittorio Emanuele II, although he was the first king of a new state, the Kingdom of Italy. Cavour was convinced, with a good degree of reason, that the other pre-1860 Italian states were governed by illiberal regimes, while Piedmont was endowed with liberal laws. He believed that liberal institutions in themselves would produce civil and economic progress. In fact, as shown in Figure 2.1, the North–South divide in GDP per capita level was to remain a permanent feature of the new state until the present day.

In 1861, less than 2 percent of Italians had the right to vote in the first Italian elections, and only half of them exercised this civil right. Many electors followed the papal instructions to boycott the new institutions. In the South, citizens felt a sense of discrimination and voted largely against the new government. Cavour had promised that the Southern regions would become the wealthiest of the kingdom within a few years, but he never traveled south of Florence. Half of the kingdom's troops were dislocated to the South to maintain public order and ruthlessly repress brigandage: the result was an increase in the local people's distance from the state's authority. The low taxation in the Bourbon State – although matched by nonexistent public services – inspired popular rebellion against the new state, in particular for its taxation on essential goods and for imposing compulsory military service. Tax evasion remained a hallmark of the economy for decades. Brigands, organized in forty large bands and numberless smaller ones, took control of many Southern districts. The most conservative representatives of the Church provided logistic assistance to some bands, which could find shelter in the Vatican State, where the former King of Naples had also hidden, and escape the repression coming from the Italian authorities. Similarly, local priests in the South sometimes sided with the brigands, who were perceived to be closer to the people than the new state. Organized crime assumed a new dimension. Statistics for 1873 reveal that in Sicily homicides were fifteen times more frequent than in Lombardy. While historians are still divided about the social and economic impact of the unification on the Southern regions, the backwardness of the *Mezzogiorno* around

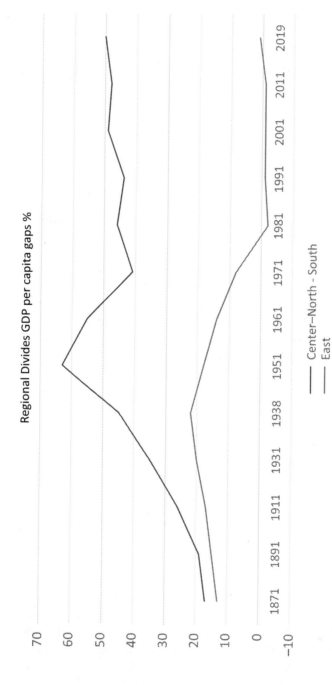

Figure 2.1 Regional divides: Percentage gaps in GDP per capita
Source: Elaborations from Iuzzolino et al. (2013: 574)

1860 was depicted in the cruelest terms by British and German visitors, some of them describing the population as subhuman, others using the much-cited picture of Naples as "a paradise inhabited by demons." British Prime Minister William Gladstone spoke of the human condition in Italy's South as a denial of God on Earth.

2.4 Causes of Delayed Catch-Up Growth

Uncertainty about the future of the Kingdom of Italy, even as an independent country, remained high in the eyes of both international and domestic public opinion, at least for the first decade after unification. On the domestic front, the situation in the South was, for at least a decade after unification, the main reason for the uncertainty surrounding the prospects of the new state. The low taxation levied by the Bourbons, and some manufacturing production around Naples and in Calabria, are often mentioned as promising signs of modernization in a landscape otherwise generally described as dominated by feudal powers and bands of thugs. The ideologically charged debate has made scholarly analysis of the impact of unification on the *Mezzogiorno* quite problematic, but what was then called "brigandage" had evidently subversive, pro-Bourbon, traits. In the 1920s, political philosopher Antonio Gramsci interpreted the fight against brigandage as an abuse of power against poor peasants and intellectuals that were "blemished as brigands, crucified, torn apart and buried alive" by the troops sent from Turin. In the first post-unification years, the heads of the public administration indeed came mostly from Piedmont. They found it so difficult to communicate with their Southern counterparts speaking local dialects that often communication between Turin and Naples or Palermo was conducted in French.

On the international front, foreign powers – except for the United Kingdom, the United States, and, somehow reluctantly, France – were slow in establishing diplomatic relations with the new kingdom. Only in late 1862, Prussia and Russia opened their embassies in Turin, while Spain waited until 1865. Full diplomatic relations with the Austrian Empire were established only in 1867. Political uncertainty was compounded by a high level of government debt, largely underwritten by foreign financial institutions. The domestic and international wait-and-see attitude about the future of the Italian state resulted in an extremely high interest rate differential between Italian and British government securities. Given such a level of uncertainty, it is hardly surprising that foreign and domestic investors did not rush to invest in the country. In 1861–1870, Italian fixed and total investment stagnated.

The steam engine was the "general purpose technology" of the time. In 1825, its employment in transportation by Stephenson aroused enthusiasm in Europe. A railway mania characterized the following decades. By 1860, Great Britain could boast 14,600 kilometers of railway track, Germany 11,000 and France 9,200. On the Italian peninsula, however, only 2,400 kilometers of railway existed in 1860, an eloquent illustration of how political and geographical fragmentation had hampered the economy before the country's unification.

The first long railway was created in the Austrian Kingdom of Lombardy-Veneto in Italy's Northeast. In 1835 the Venetian Chamber of Commerce approved a project[6] to link by rail Milan and Venice, the kingdom's two capitals. Considered at the time an under-taking of epic dimensions for its length, the construction of the Milan–Venice railway was strewn with pitfalls and complications, including fierce international controversies, judicial, bureaucratic and political interventions involving Vienna's authorities. It took twenty-two years to complete the 288 kilometers of the "Ferdinandea" railway, named in honor of Austrian Emperor Ferdinand I. It became fully operative only after Italy's unification.

The Kingdom of Sardinia promoted the construction of new lines and studied the extension to the rest of the peninsula in accordance with the Savoyard plans to unite the country. The first railway between Turin and Genoa formed a large detour west of the city of Alessandria, a link that, once expanded to Milan, created the cradle for Italy's twentieth-century industrial triangle. Pope Gregory XVI significantly opposed the railways, which could have rapidly transported troops from Northern powers into the Papal State. Moreover, Italy's moun-tainous geography required huge investments to lay down the rails or dig, sometimes by hand, the tunnels through the Apennines. Consequently, the expensive work had to be funded by international capital, giving foreign powers a strong voice in Italy's railway invest-ments. Even Giuseppe Garibaldi, briefly dictator in Naples, personally saw that in every single kingdom of the Italian peninsula, local or international political considerations prevailed over the centralized plans for modernizing transportation and the economy. Considerable progress was made between 1850 and 1860, bringing the length of rail tracks from 371 to 2,238 kilometers, two-thirds of which were in Northern Italy. However, the gap with the main European countries remained enormous.

Yet, the new state was surprisingly efficient in creating a railway network, especially given the country's mountainous terrain. Rail lines were built along the Adriatic and Tyrrhenian coasts and across the Apennines. In 1867, Italy was first linked to Northern Europe through the Brenner Pass. In 1871 the first Frejus tunnel was opened, connecting Italy to France. Besides the Suez Canal, it was the most daring work of transport engineering of its time. The Gottardo and Simplon lines followed. As a result of the hectic railway building, the rail network almost quadrupled by 1880 to 9,290 kilometers. However, the creation of the main railway lines was a necessary but not entirely sufficient condition for the unification of the Italian market. For the rail system to be efficient, it required the construction of "secondary" lines linking provincial market cities to the main network (Fenoaltea 1983).

Cheap transportation was a key element in exploiting the potential advantages of a large single market created by Italy's political unification. Equally important was the actual implementation of national financial, monetary and legal regimes. Parliamentary laws were sufficient for the formal (*de jure*) unification of the currency, weights and measures, and for economic legislation, but their actual (de facto) unification was quite a different matter. Centuries of political fragmentation had cemented the local monetary, banking and business habits. They could not be unified at the stroke of a pen. A tourist visiting a medieval Italian city around 1860 would find, in the old marketplace, weights and measures applied to every transaction visibly engraved in stone. Moving to the next town he would find a similar engraving, except that, for instance, the length of the "arm" (a measure of lengths) in one market would be different from the other. Consequently, intercity or interstate contracts were required to specify which city's weights and measures applied to each particular transaction (e.g., "arms of Siena," "of Florence," etc.). A merchant's trading skills included knowledge of the weights and measures of each Italian market they did business with. More important still was for a merchant to master the exchange rates of the various coins in circulation and the bookkeeping procedures of each Italian state.

The decimal system was introduced soon after unification, but it took several years for every single municipality to abandon the use of its traditional weights and measures, which differed from those with the same name even in neighboring villages. In 1875, Italy participated in the creation of the International Bureau of Weights and Measures. In 1877, a Royal Decree established "tables" for the conversion of the local measures into single national ones based on the decimal system. Only in 1890 did a comprehensive law settle and clarify all the legal aspects of weights and measures.

In August 1862, the "Italian lira" was born when the "Savoy lira" became the official currency of the kingdom and exchange rates and deadlines were established for the conversion of the old states' currencies into the new single one. The Italian lira was exchanged at par with the French franc. The bimetallic system was adopted whereby banknotes could be converted into gold or silver at a fixed exchange rate between the two metals. If, after 1999, the transition from individual national currencies of the European countries to the euro took only three years to be effectively completed, the full substitution of the currencies of the old states on the peninsula by the Italian lira took much longer. In the first decade after the unification, uncertainty about the future of the new state made people cautious about changing their money into the new currency, but the main reason why it took such a long time for monetary unification is to be found in the intrinsic metal (mostly silver) value of the old coins, which made up about 70 percent of the entire circulation, as banknotes and bank deposits only slowly increased their share in the total money supply. The citizens of the new kingdom had no incentive to convert the old currencies into the new one as the old ones retained their metallic value and, as such, continued to be accepted in local markets where they had been in use for centuries or were hoarded to preserve the value of citizens', particularly peasants', savings. It is no wonder that by 1870 only 57 percent of the pre-1861 monetary stock had been converted into lire. Only in 1894, was the last stock of coins from the Kingdom of the Two Sicilies brought to the mint to be converted into lire (De Mattia 1959).

A banking union was also extremely slow in being established.[7] The banks of issue of the pre-unification states, owned by the local financial elites, fought hard to maintain their privileges and shares in the regional markets. It was not until 1894 that four of those banks were consolidated into one, the Bank of Italy, to form an embryonic central bank. The unification of the stock market did not take place until the 1880s (Toniolo et al. 2003). Here again, interests coalesced around the local stock exchanges and played an important role in slowing down the process.

The unification of the relevant legal institutions took a longer time than optimists had expected in 1861 (Bianco and Napolitano 2013). A Civil Code and a Commercial Code were instituted by Parliament in 1865. The former had a clear French imprint while the latter derived, with minor modifications, from previous Piedmont trade legislation and did not take into account the most recent business practices. Only in 1882, a new Commercial Code was launched, based on the revolutionary idea that, in economic matters, commercial regulations should prevail over civil ones. Unfortunately, however, administrative rules and the national bureaucracy did not prove to be fully up to the task of promoting economic development. It will be one of those ancient flaws from which the country will never be able to heal. Despite all this, around the 1880s the country could benefit from new infrastructures and institutions reducing the obstacles that had stood in the way of economic development.

The new kingdom proved quite successful in creating the necessary physical infrastructure to exploit the relatively large single market and its connection to the rest of Europe. Unfortunately, it was not equally successful in addressing one of the most economically and socially damaging legacies of the old states: educational poverty. While the most recent literature on the successes and failures in economic growth largely focuses on institutions, for Abramovitz (1989) in the "social capability for growth" (or lack thereof) education plays a key role. In 1861, Piedmont had a literacy rate of 50.6 percent of the population, the highest among the Italian regions. The Savoy monarchy had done a good job in its mainland domains (less so in Liguria), but had neglected Sardinia, at the time the least educated among the Italian regions. In Lombardy, the school system of the hated Austrian oppressor had succeeded in reaching a 48.7 percent literacy rate, while Veneto lagged behind, with 36.3 percent in 1870. The Bourbon kings had been particularly negligent in educating their subjects since, in their former continental domains, only 15 percent of the population could read and write. Sicily was in an even worse condition. The popes provided better education for their subjects living in Latium, around Rome, than the inhabitants of the rest of their domains, including the

Northern region around Bologna. Illiteracy in the South was the product of absolutist domination. Throughout the Italian peninsula, most
social interventions, including education and housing, were not undertaken directly by the state with apt legislation and administration but
rather by individuals and mostly Catholic charities of goodwill that
operated according to their discretionary objectives, only slightly over-
seen and regulated by the state. The dependence on the goodwill and
the initiative of the rich and powerful may have been partly responsible
for the widespread eagerness of the ordinary people to win their
benevolence.

In November 1861, Parliament extended to the whole Kingdom of
Italy a Piedmont law from 1859 regulating the education system of the
country. Elementary (primary) education was divided into two cycles
of two years each. Primary school attendance was compulsory and free
for all Italian children aged six to nine. However, no provisions for the
enforcement of the obligation existed, nor incentives for parents to
send children to school rather than to work. Moreover, it was up to the
municipal authorities to provide for both classrooms and teachers. As
local communities were generally underfunded, the provision of public
schools was uneven across the country and in some remote places
simply did not exist. Local clerical and conservative elites did not
consider the mass diffusion of education useful or, in any case, a
priority. In such conditions, primary school enrollment increased from
44.7 percent in 1861 to 77.5 percent in 1901, with a large gap between
the Center–North (93.7 percent in 1901) and the South (52.6 percent
in 1901) (Vecchi 2017: table 5.A3). In 1890, 25 percent of noncom-
pliance with compulsory education was due to poverty and 20 percent
to difficulties in accessing the school, again with wide discrepancies
across regions (Vecchi 2017: 198). Only in the first decade of the
twentieth century, the cost of compulsory education was taken up by
the national government.

In the fifteen–nineteen age group, literacy (the share of the population able to read and write) grew from a meager 27 percent in 1861 to
61 percent in 1911 (Vecchi 2017: table 5. A). That was relatively rapid
progress, but insufficient to equip the country with an adequately
educated workforce. The fact that Italy was a relatively poor country
does not absolve its elites from what Tullio De Mauro called their
"mortal sin": neglecting education, a form of negligence that unfortunately remained endemic in the country's entire successive history. In

comparison, Japan, with a lower per capita income than Italy in 1860, and starting from a lower level of school participation, by 1910 reached a participation rate considered by scholars to be the maximum achievable at the time and a literacy rate higher than Italy's (Vecchi 2017: 201–202).

The low priority given to education by post-unitary governments is attributable to various causes including the hostility of Catholics to compulsory state education, one of the poisoned fruits of the already mentioned exclusion of large segments of the population from the process constructing national unity.

The low school expenditure also depended on public finance constraints. The new state was born with a public debt-to-GDP ratio of around 40 percent. The decision to honor the debt of all pre-unification states favored especially Piedmont. In the so-called preparatory decade, the Savoy kingdom had deficit-financed both public works and the buttressing of its army. Moreover, Italy's debt was very expensive, also due to the abovementioned markets' skepticism about the unitary process. On average, between 1861 and 1894, despite a decrease in the spread (Fig. 2.2), 37 percent of total government expenditure was dedicated to servicing the debt (net interest and repayments). Military expenditure (20 percent of the total), a domain of the Crown, was deemed incompressible, as were those for the basic state functions (administration, justice and public safety, 24 percent of the total). Discretionary expenses, including public investments, were, therefore, a mere quarter of the total. With little foresight, only 2 percent of public expenditure was allocated to education (Bastasin et al. 2019).

2.5 *"E Pur Si Muove"* (And Yet It Moves)

Galileo's alleged reply to the Inquisition about the earth not staying still may also apply to Italy's history. The previous pages focused on the structural and contingent shortcomings of the new Kingdom of Italy, mainly to explain the reasons why political unification did not immediately fulfill the economic expectations of the Risorgimento's founding fathers. The reader may thus be left with the impression that nothing good came from the unification, at least as far as social and economic conditions were concerned. We now need to rectify that negative impression.

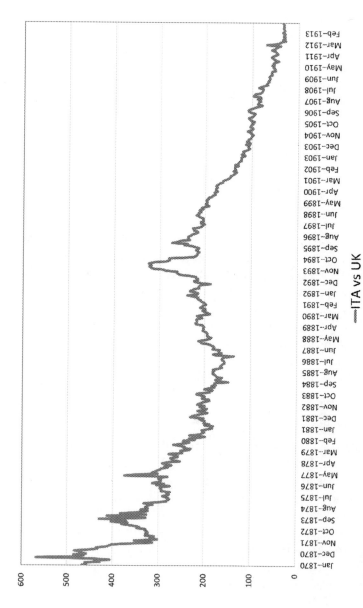

Figure 2.2 Interest rate differential (basis points) between Italian and British government perpetual bonds
Source: Toniolo 2022

While the pre-unification divergence trend from the richest European countries was not reversed, the Italian economy was nonetheless growing. Even though, as we have seen, the GDP growth rate was moderate, the compound interest magic was at work: In 1894, the real income per capita was 21 percent higher than at the time of the unification. Over the same period, the average height of recruits, a good indicator of overall well-being, increased by 2 centimeters; personal income inequality and absolute poverty were slightly reduced, and the plague of child labor considerably diminished. The average Italian was not undernourished and increased his or her calorie availability by about 10 percent. All regions benefited from these trends, albeit at a different pace: The North–South gap widened.

Between 1861 and 1873, the GDP grew by only 0.7 percent per annum, barely enough to match the population growth. We have already seen the reasons for the wait-and-see attitude of domestic and foreign investors. The 1866 war coincided with an international financial crisis. Prudential reasons and wartime financial needs suggested suspending the metal convertibility of the Italian lira. It was only resumed in 1883. The exchange rate devaluation provided a welcome boost to the export sector but held back investment and private consumption growth. As an unintended consequence, the suspension of convertibility favored the circulation of paper money denominated in the Italian lira, accelerating the progress of monetary unification.

The international financial crisis of 1873 highlighted the weakness of the monetary and banking system, soliciting a response from the Italian Parliament. In 1874 the first comprehensive banking law was passed: The six banks of issue were better regulated and a clearinghouse was created for the settlement of their mutual balances. With the transfer of the capital city to Rome, its final location, uncertainty about the stability of the new kingdom abated, both at home and abroad. From the second half of the 1870s, both GDP and investment picked up. Between 1875 and 1888, GDP grew at an annual compound rate of 1.6 percent and fixed investments by as much as 3.9 percent. A large steelmaking plant was established in Terni, mainly for the supply of the expanding shipbuilding and arms industries. Foreign capital inflow accelerated with the return to gold convertibility of the lira in 1883. This turned out to be a mixed blessing. To make the gold standard commitment credible, the government subscribed to a large gold-denominated foreign debt, which increased the metal reserves of the banks of issue.

Larger reserves allowed the banks to increase circulation and industrial credit at moderate interest rates. A part of bank finance went to investments in manufacturing industries, but a large segment went to the construction industry, creating the condition of the financial crisis described in Chapter 3. In addition, a huge demand for credit came from the construction sector. Rome, the new capital, needed a rapid expansion of government office space and housing for the civil servants and their families who were flooding the Eternal City. Construction renewal plans were also underway in Turin and Naples. Demand for mortgages was generously accommodated by small and large banks, including banks of issue: We shall see in the next chapter how excessive risk-taking by credit institutions led to a major financial crisis.

We have already said that the new state was born with a public debt equal to about 40 percent of its GDP. Even by the time's financial orthodoxy standards, it was not exceedingly high. The problem was that, in 1862, tax revenues covered only about half of government expenditure. The extension of Piedmont's tax laws to the whole country made Italy one of the European countries with the highest tax-to-GDP ratio, which added to the discontent, particularly in the South where the Bourbon's fiscal policy had been based on the principle of low taxes and low expenditure. Further tax hikes were thus out of the question. At the same time, as mentioned above, expenditure proved impossible to be reduced, given the rigidity of most items in the state budget. Nonetheless, in 1864–1865, Quintino Sella, a finance minister still remembered today for his unflinching financial orthodoxy (his work desk is still kept as a memento at the Finance Ministry), tried to increase revenues and reduce expenditures. His attempts failed because the 1865 secret government commitment to join Prussia against Austria required an expansion of military outlays. The following war brought the debt-to-GDP ratio close to 100 percent. In 1862 the state had taken possession of the lands owned by the religious orders, which were subsequently auctioned. This measure of extraordinary finance enriched several private individuals while bringing limited benefits to public finance. A broad-based and easily collectible tax was introduced: the grist tax collected directly at the mills. Taxation of bond yields was also implemented. In his second stint as finance minister (1869–1873), Sella took "a series of measures aimed mainly at improving efficiency in tax collection, which raised state revenue by almost 20 percent, and brought the deficit down to only 1 percent of GDP" (Toniolo 2015:

p. 63). The debt-to-GDP ratio fell to 80 percent in 1874. But it then resumed growing despite the tight fiscal policy pursued by the governments of the "historical right-wing," which in 1876 could boast a balanced budget. In the following years, governments were led by a self-styled "left-wing" political aggregation. It should be said that a large consensus existed in the post-Risorgimento political elite on "sound public finance" principles. Deficit spending remained relatively limited but slow GDP growth and high rates of interest on government borrowing produced a series of primary deficits, which, with some interruptions, generated an upward trend in debt-to-GDP ratios, reaching 125 percent in 1894 (Fig. 2.3).

Before moving on in the next chapter to Italy's secular convergence with the high-income countries, a few words must be said on tariff policy. Cavour and the other founding fathers, particularly those from Piedmont and Tuscany, were convinced free traders. In 1861, the extension of Piedmont's tariff was conducted without providing time to adjust to the previously highly protected areas, particularly those in the former Kingdom of the Two Sicilies. Foreign and Northern competition hit the South's unprepared industrial sector hard. Italian exports more than doubled in real terms between 1861 and 1887 but the foreign trade balance remained negative throughout the period. Foreign price competition to Italian wheat growers increased as transatlantic transportation costs steadily diminished. In 1887, political tension with France over Tunisia led to a "tariff war" with Paris, which was particularly damaging to Italian wine production. Agrarian interests sought higher protection. As they did not command a parliamentary majority to pass a new tariff law, landowners made an agreement with representatives of the largest manufacturing industry for a substantial increase in the import duties on both wheat and steel, incorporated in the 1887 tariff law. A pact dubbed the "marriage of iron and rye" had been struck eight years earlier in Germany between the Junkers and representatives of the iron and steel manufacturers. Free traders, both in Germany and Italy, had no doubts in defining such an unnatural alliance of vested interests as "pactum sceleris" (criminal agreement) or unholy alliance. The Italian tariff of 1887 protected two sectors in which the country had no comparative (or even absolute) advantage, while at the same time reinvigorating the political and social clout of the Southern latifundia owners, much as the 1879 Reich's tariff upheld the power of the Prussian large landowners.

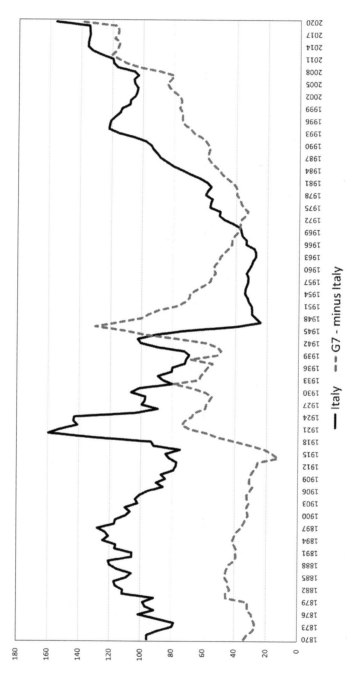

Figure 2.3 Gross public debt, percentage of GDP 1870–2020
G7 data refer to an average weighted on national GDP.
Sources of data: IMF (2021), Maddison, (2018), WEO Database.

—— Italy   - - - G7 - minus Italy

3 | Convergence and Sorpasso

3.1 Catching Up (Belatedly) with the "First Globalization": The Credibility Issue

In 1893–1894, Italy underwent one of the most serious political and financial crises in its history, and in 1896 it abandoned the costly imperialist ambitions in Ethiopia after a bloody defeat. These events were followed by a spell of growth acceleration. This chapter describes the combination of the vitalism of Italy's economy, the impulse from the international context and the predicaments of public life in the various historical periods that characterize the secular convergence of Italy's GDP per capita with the most advanced countries.

In 1896, Italy's per capita income saw the largest divergence from the other Western countries. Italy's GDP was only 38 percent of that of the United Kingdom and 60 percent of that of France. Less than two decades later, the distance had shrunk. In 1913, Italian per capita GDP rose to 52 and 73 percent, respectively, of the British and French ones (Table 1.2). The centuries-old gap with the Western European countries did not only stop widening but it began to narrow. Only compared to the United States (then a rapidly growing "emerging country" that attracted workers and capital in large quantities) did the distance remain almost unchanged.

About a fifth of the new growth may be attributed to the international cyclical upswing, but the rest was the consequence of structural improvement (Ciocca 2007: 142–143). Between 1896 and 1913, the average annual growth of aggregate and per capita incomes was 2.4 and 1.6 percent, respectively. Beginning in the 1880s, the modern and most dynamic sectors saw a surge in productivity growth (product per worker) that accelerated during the "Giolitti age" (roughly the decade between 1901 and 1911, named after Prime Minister Giovanni Giolitti), reaching 2.5 percent per year in the industrial sector. Between 1881 and 1911, labor productivity of the entire economy increased on average 1.3 percent annually, as much as in the United States and much more than in the United Kingdom, against a modest 0.4 percent in the previous twenty years (Broadberry et al. 2013).

The turning point, the discontinuity, in Italy's post-unification economic growth can be dated around the mid-1890s. At the end of the previous decade, the inflow of gold into the country had stopped, partly due to overtrading by the banking sector and also caused by a trade war with France. In that case, Italy's international reputation was not helped by its sudden change in military alliances, from London and Paris to Berlin and Vienna. Italian banks were forced to reduce their exposure, particularly to the construction sector, piercing a bubble inflated in the previous years by easy credit and rising real estate prices. The least financially solid construction companies went bust, and contagion spread first to the smaller and then to the larger banks, along a typical mechanism seen at work many other times in the history of international financial crises. The largest bank of issue, Banca Nazionale del Regno, could not supply lending of last resort due to its own inadequate liquidity. As is often the case in such circumstances, the banking crisis was compounded by criminal behavior and political scandals. By 1892–1893, most Italian banks were either illiquid or insolvent. The crisis dragged on until the eleventh hour when the government stepped in: Four banks of issue were consolidated into the new Bank of Italy, today's Italian central bank. In 1894–1895, the two largest commercial banks, both of French origin, were liquidated. Their place was taken by two new banks, with considerable German input of both capital and management. The birth of an embryonic central bank and the reorganization on sounder bases of the banking sector put an end to the panic and laid the economic foundation for growth acceleration (Toniolo 2022). Political foundations, meanwhile, had to wait for a military defeat in Ethiopia (1896), which put an end to Italy's delayed imperial ambitions. After a brief spell of reactionary governments, the new political leadership was based on personalities, especially Giolitti, who pursued social inclusion and growth-friendly monetary and fiscal policies. Political ostracism of Socialists and Catholics was progressively abandoned, as was the hard confrontation with the emerging trade unions. On the economic front, credible time-consistent monetary and fiscal policies were sustained over the long term. The new policies were based on debt consolidation, foreign exchange stability and lower interest rates. Foreign and domestic investment, which had been repelled by the high uncertainty of 1887–1894, found its way back to Italy.

Italy's industrial modernization began in earnest a few decades later than in the neighboring countries, as anyone could see when traveling from Rome to London, Paris or Vienna. At the end of the nineteenth century, both the French and the Austrian capitals[1] were going through an age of aesthetic greatness that went down in history as the *belle époque*. Rome had last been renovated in the seventeenth century by Pope Alessandro VII and his two architects, fierce rivals, Bernini and Borromini, made the holy city a destination for pilgrims from all over Europe. In 1871, when it became the capital of the new Kingdom of Italy, Rome was neither a large metropolis (it had fewer inhabitants than Naples or Milan) nor a city that developed an autochthonous bourgeoisie through the promotion of the lower classes. After Rome became the country's capital, speculative real estate developers, who were often invited from Piedmont by the new administrators and who were at the origin of the financial crisis of 1892–1894, changed the city's urban profile, while a large bureaucracy, often coming from the Southern regions, grew out of proportion with the tiny private economy.

Italian industrialization matured, mostly in the Northwest of the country, within the technological context of the Second Industrial Revolution. Industrial production, which in 1896 contributed only to one-sixth of GDP (with no change from 1871), rose to one-fourth in 1913. The greatest expansion occurred in the manufacturing sector, excluding buildings and mines, with double-digit growth rates in the metallurgical and electromechanical industries and in the production of hydroelectric energy, which in Italy reached diffusion and technical levels among the first in Europe (Gomellini and Toniolo 2017). Large companies were created whose names are still alive and well-known today: Fiat, Pirelli, Ansaldo, Falck, Ilva. The new largest banks, the Banca Commerciale Italiana and the Credito Italiano, not only established greater links with the increasingly integrated international capital markets but also introduced the "universal bank" model in Italy, which promoted new businesses, mergers, business combinations and capital placement of stocks listed on the Milan Stock Exchange. The latter developed rapidly both in the number and capitalization of the listed companies.

Italy's post-1896 growth took place in the international environment of the "first globalization" in which Italians could finally fully participate. Between 1896 and 1911, exports grew by 4 percent a year, much faster than the GDP, and imports by 5 percent. The deficit in the external trade balance was easily financed by remittances from emigrants and by tourism, so much so that toward the end of the period the balance of payments was often in surplus, generating a small but significant flow of investments abroad. Together with the import of machinery, direct foreign investments by Italian companies were the main vehicles for the acquisition of the most advanced technology, a typical way through which the least developed countries manage to grow faster than the richer ones.

This first phase of rapid growth and convergence introduced a long-lasting policy variable in Italy's history that is still relevant today: the "external credibility" issue. As we have seen, in the 1880s, the Kingdom of Italy gained more trust among foreign governments and markets, only to lose it again in the early 1890s. In an interesting parallel with the first decades of the euro's history, it took twenty years for unified Italy to no longer be seen as a precarious artifact at risk of dissolution. Against a backdrop of relatively high public debt and interest rates, Italian governments learned to be careful in pleasing foreign lenders, sometimes more than they pleased the Italian citizens. From the late 1890s onward, the Italian economy hugely benefited from the country's regained and growing external credibility.

The gap between politics and popular sentiment, however, remained wide. Between 1871 and 1914, 14 million Italians emigrated in search of better living conditions. Eight million left after 1901 when the Italian economy was growing faster. Many originated from the Southern regions where labor was not organized, and workers were often badly exploited. In 1898, revolts spread in many cities throughout the country protesting the high price of bread and the lack of jobs. Some riots, notably in Milan, were repressed with violence and resulted in many deaths. The press was in the hands of industrial interests willing to exert pressure on politics, a degradation of civil rights and freedoms that is still visible today.

During the first phase of Italy's economic convergence with the more advanced countries, the economic institutions grew stronger. The single market took hold both on commerce and on the financial sector. Rail and road networks grew both in size and quality. Harbors, essential to an open economy, were enlarged and modernized. The Italian language began to spread beyond the thin layer of the educated bourgeoisie. The banking sector was consolidated, and its fragility reduced with the formation of a more credible lender of last resort, such as the Bank of England and the Bank of France had been for decades. During the international financial crisis of 1907, which originated on Wall Street, the danger of major bank failure was aptly defused by the Bank of Italy, enhancing its new reputation as a guarantor of financial stability, which, together with macroeconomic (monetary and fiscal) stability provided by successive governments, reduced uncertainty for those, Italians or foreigners, interested in investing in Italy and for emigrants who placed their savings in a solid currency. Despite the fast rotation of governments, which is another persistent Italian anomaly, the commitment to a stable currency and public finances was never in dispute. The convertibility of the lira into gold, suspended in 1894 at the height of the banking crisis, was not officially resumed, but throughout the period the monetary authorities consistently followed the strategy of mimicking the gold standard "as if" the lira were convertible. The currency remained stable at 25 lire per pound and one lira per French franc. This was a clever policy, as speculators could not bet without risk against the lira, whose value instead remained credibly stable for the markets (Cesarano et al. 2012).

Monetary policy was accompanied by an equally credible commitment to a slow but steady reduction in the public debt-to-GDP ratio, which was reduced from 125 percent in 1894, the highest peacetime level before the 2008–2013 crisis, to 75 percent in 1913. Divided and quarrelsome then as now, the economic and political elites were nonetheless united in believing that a high public debt slowed economic growth, limited the margin of maneuver of economic policy and weakened the country's independence. Even without sticking to a rigorous budget balance, Italian governments consistently maintained what we today call "primary surpluses" (positive public budget balances net of interest expenditure). In the late 1890s, this policy resulted in limited "austerity," but then the combination of GDP growth and the reduction of interest rates on government securities produced a virtuous circle: debt reduction – lower interest rates – higher nominal GDP growth – further reduction of the debt-to-GDP ratio, which made it possible to increase public spending to conduct the more socially inclusive policies characterizing the Giolitti age.

We have already stressed that, throughout Italy's post-unification history, successive governments resorted to public expenditure to appease deep internal divisions, often ending up increasing public debt and reducing the country's external credibility. At the beginning of the twentieth century, however, the tacit but consistent commitment to solid public finance in a context of rapidly growing GDP made it possible for interest rates on Italian securities to fall faster than in any other advanced country. In 1893, the spread (interest rate differential) on Italian long-term securities compared to the English ones had reached 325 basis points, while in January 1913 it was only 31 basis points, a level lower than that of Germany, the United States and Russia. In 1913, only one-tenth of Italy's public debt was held abroad, although public spending, which increased in nominal terms by almost 5 percent annually, was among the highest in Europe.

The increase in the average lifespan continued. In 1911, life expectancy at birth reached the French level (45 years). The gap with Sweden, then the European country with the longest living population, was also considerably reduced (Vecchi 2017: 92). The average height of recruits continued to increase (Vecchi 2017: 57). Such significant improvements were directly attributable to state investments in sewer systems, aqueducts, hospitals and school buildings, as well as to the diffusion of *medici condotti* – local doctors in the countryside with sanitation expertise, especially in bacteriology. Infant mortality decreased together with the decline of deaths attributable to infectious, respiratory and gastroenteric diseases (Vecchi 2017: 97). Malaria, which in 1901 still caused forty-two deaths per 100,000 inhabitants, was reduced to only 10 in 1911 (Vecchi 2017: 102). Literacy and the ability to perform elementary arithmetic operations continued to grow.

Seen in the light of previous "industrial revolutions," this late Italian manufacturing and GDP upswing had a peculiarly "benevolent" character (Toniolo 2003), as it benefited low-income, even poor, citizens more than the rest of the population. Recent research shows that a reduction in income distribution inequality took place in those years (Vecchi 2017: 313–321), albeit from high levels. This peculiarity of Italy's "industrial revolution" is relevant from this book's perspective. It is hard to say whether inequality reduction simply coincided with or was driven by stronger economic growth. But it certainly began to produce a more homogeneous society, which contributed to the country's stability, therefore producing positive results from investments and growth.

Our present knowledge allows us only to hypothesize about the causes of the relative "benevolence" of Italy's "industrial revolution" compared to the English one of the early nineteenth century. Among the hypotheses, two are the most plausible, and they are both related to the international environment. On the one hand, it was the less wealthy population that benefited most from the fruits of the second industrial revolution: the spread of electricity and drinking water in homes, the cities' improved sanitation and cheaper public transport. On the other hand, in the least developed European countries, the "first globalization" tended to redistribute income in favor of wage earners, especially those with low qualifications. The collapse in international transport costs brought cheap grain also to Italy. The price of bread, still a key item in the diet of the less well-off, decreased, increasing the purchasing power of wages. More controversially, emigration – also facilitated by the collapse of transport costs – took the least qualified workers out of Italy, increasing the average wage of those who remained.

Given that globalization necessarily changes the distribution of income (today we speak somewhat vulgarly about winners and losers), in the pre-1914 internationalization of the Italian economy, wage earners, rather than holders of real or financial wealth, were the main "winners." The inclusion, albeit late, of Italy in the "first globalization," therefore, not only accelerated per capita income growth but made its distribution slightly less unfair.

The development of the market economy was faster than the state-building process. We have already argued that in Italy the state-citizens gap was larger than in the neighboring countries, with a long history as nation-states. While growing, the average level of education in Italy was lower than in Northwestern Europe, and the extension of the electoral franchise also proceeded at a slower pace, as did the electoral participation of those who had the right to vote. The large economic gap between the Northwest of the country and the South increased after unification, adding to a diminished sense of common statehood. As a result, on the one hand, citizens mistrusted the state, but on the other, the state itself dictated the exclusion of most people from political participation.

The unification was carried out by discarding the ideas purported by Risorgimento leaders such as Mazzini, who claimed that "the Italian people should decide, as a national community, freely, directly and in full" on their political regime. Rather than a "national pact" dictated by the constituency, continuity with the Kingdom of Sardinia pre-vailed. The Italian national–popular cause of the Risorgimento morphed into a monarchical government organization. While a few years earlier the French adopted a constitution voted by popular assemblies and the German Reichstag adopted a constitution in 1867 (modified in 1871), "in Italy the population did not participate in any way in the configuration that the new state would have to assume" (Cassese 2019: 21).[2] Mazzini concluded that united Italy was only a ghost because it lacked the soul of a nation.

Participation in political life remained low. The percentage of the population admitted to exercising the right to vote never overcame 2 percent in the first twenty years (1861–1881). It oscillated between 6 and 9 percent in the following thirty years (1882–1909) and rose to around 30 percent in the ten years between 1913 and 1923.[3] From 1864 to 1877, five proposals for electoral reform were presented but were not even discussed. In 1882, after six years of government by the Left, suffrage was increased to 2 million voters (Italy's population was, in the meantime, about 30 million). In 1912 the "universal" suffrage (male only) was introduced.

Around the turn of the twentieth century, the zeitgeist changed throughout Europe. The fall in the credibility of the nineteenth century liberal–democratic model occurred in parallel with the great trans-formations affecting European society.[4]

Between the aspiration of the Italian people and the discredit of the institutions, tension built up when the Kingdom engaged in a string of bellicose adventures that all ended badly and are likely to have contrib-uted to the explosive sentiments that resulted in the fascist movement after World War I. In 1866, the Third Italian War of Independence against Austria ended in two defeats that historians ascribe to crass disorganization and internecine conflicts within Piedmont's military hierarchy. The war against the Ethiopian Empire between 1885 and 1896 produced more tragic defeats in Dogali, Amba Alagi and Adua. Even the conquest of Libya between 1911 and 1915 eventually brought limited results after the loss of control of the rebellious terri-tories in Tripolitania with severe implications for the Italian army. If wars contribute to the formation of the state, it should not be a surprise that Italians have remained suspicious of public institutions. Wars need huge organizational apparatuses that expand to the private sectors through provisions, transport, public contracts, industrial delivery, etc. On the one hand, during wartime, the state contributes more than ever to imposing order on society, spreading the culture of organized activity through hierarchy, obedience, mutual respect, procedures and timely interaction. On the other hand, to accomplish this, the state requires popular support and a certain degree of social consensus.[5]

The intervention of the state in the allocation of economic resources, investment in particular, began soon after unification, as mentioned in Chapter 2. The main instruments were subsidies, procurement, import duties and public works. In this respect, Italy was not different from other European countries such as France and Germany. Peculiar, however, was the weakness of Italy's public administration. Only in 1878, a Ministry of Agriculture, Industry and Trade was established, though it was thinly staffed and with limited competencies.

As in the case of 1887, several state interventions were originally intended to promote import-substituting industries but also ended up making export sectors less competitive, often at the cost of the newly developing industries in the South, thus increasing the dualism of the Italian economy. The import duty on wheat and corn also strengthened the grain-producing latifundia. The 1887 tariff law was never repealed but, after 1900, its negative impact on the economy was considerably mitigated when Italy signed several commercial treaties with other countries aimed at reciprocally reducing import duties (Toniolo 1977). Customs protection developed in parallel with public subsidies to individual industries or private firms, particularly in shipbuilding, maritime transport and defense-related industries. Moreover, as common in other countries, several cartels were created with the blessing of the government, primarily in the cotton, silk and steel sectors.

Other aspects of the state's intervention in the Italian economy influenced the future development of the economic system. One of them is related to infrastructural investments in less developed areas. These entailed the introduction of special procedures (for example, the expropriation procedure for Naples); the establishment of special bodies (regional superintendents for public works); providing relief, tax reductions and subsidized or guaranteed credits; and subrogation of legally compulsory contractual clauses to voluntary contractual clauses, discriminatory taxation, tariff concessions and grants in favor of specific areas of the national territory. All these increased the political discretionary powers and the direct links between politicians and individual firms.

Public intervention was essential but not always efficient for the creation of public infrastructures (roads, railways, harbors, telegraph and telephone lines) and services, many of them subject to state regulation and supervision, something that exposed the inadequacy of the public administration. State intervention began soon after unification, but gradually developed in the following decades, with the tendency to subject the private management of relevant services to state's "reserve," increasing the political power over relevant economic activities. Not every act of state intervention in the economy had negative effects. Since the unification, the railway system was run on state concession by three main private companies. The service, however, was far from efficient, also due to the low incentives to invest. In 1905, most railways were nationalized and run by a state-owned company. The service became more efficient (or less inefficient) than it had previously been.

The third area of state intervention in the economy was of a social character: the first steps toward the creation of a welfare state, which would only take modern form after WWII. Italy lagged behind Germany and the United Kingdom in providing forms of social welfare. The first law for the public provision of some health services was approved in 1888. Ten years later a semi-public national pension fund was established (Giorgi and Pavan 2021). The 1901 law on emigration also provided for some form of assistance. It was only during and after WWI that the demand for more comprehensive forms of social security received new attention. Even then, however, welfare provisions remained largely in the hands of private initiatives, often organized by the Church, mainly through the 27,000 *opere pie*, the charitable organizations active in 1900. The state was expected at most to regulate and supervise those initiatives. Consequently, the welfare system was limited, segmented and very heterogeneous, feeding a sense of injustice among the population.

In the decade before the outbreak of WWI, Giolitti strived quite successfully to integrate Catholic and Socialist movements into political life, eventually leading to an (almost) universal extension of the right to vote (the so-called franchise) to the entire male population. In due time, particularly during the war and the Great Depression of the 1930s, universal male suffrage contributed to increasing the role of the state in the economy, eventually consolidating as a permanent feature of Italy's socioeconomic "material constitution," supported by a large consensus. Revealingly, since the beginning of the twentieth century, Italy has been characterized by the coexistence of two polarized political orientations, the Catholic and the Socialist, sharing a common inclination to expand the role of the state, while at the same time careful to preserve the country's external credibility. In this context, it is not surprising that Giolitti appointed some non-partisan experts as ministers in his cabinets, a first sign of the technocratic rebalancing act that characterized several moments in Italy's political economy and public life in the following century.

3.2 The Catch-Up Pace Slows Down, 1914–1939

Between the beginning of the Great War and the end of the second and even more devastating world conflict, Europe went through a most dramatic period, which was dubbed by John Maynard Keynes as "the second Thirty Years' War." Blood and destruction seemed to herald the end of Europe as a beacon of civilization, the fatherland of reason and philosophy, highlighting instead the features of Europe's history molded by tribalism, violence and colonial crimes. War and tyranny obscured the light of reason. Italy had anticipated the moment, being the first country with a fascist dictatorship. The reasons for the collapse of democracy in 1922 are still debated by historians. Several of them focused on how the transformation of Italian society and economy was conducive to the conquest of power by a dictator.

Italy joined the Triple Entente only in 1915, still somewhat under the illusion of a relatively brief conflict. The year 1914 had seen a recession, but in the autumn of the following year, industrial production recovered to the 1913 levels, which were maintained throughout the war. What mattered for subsequent development was the "industrial mobilization" for military production: Steelmaking, shipbuilding, heavy engineering and chemical industries – all heavily subsidized – underwent rapid expansion, at the expense of the consumer goods sectors. Of special importance for postwar economic growth was the expansion of the hydroelectric power industry, which was a particularly advanced sector in Italy already before the war. The aeronautical industry saw promising developments, and mass production of automotive vehicles created the basis for peacetime progress. Italy's participation in WWI had its successes and failures. On the positive side, Italy ended the war with a military victory and an economy that was largely

intact: The economic mobilization did not bring about economic collapse, and that alone, for a country of Italy's developmental level, was
a "substantial achievement" (Harrison and Galssi 2005:303). Overall,
the Italian economy held up quite well to the war effort: In 1918 the
Italian GDP was roughly equal to that of 1914, while France and
Germany lost about a third of theirs (Broadberry 2005).

Financing the war left a negative legacy. Between 1913 and 1918,
public expenditure rose from 11 to 37 percent of GDP. Taxation
covered only 16 percent of the war-related government outlays; the
rest came from debt (both domestic and foreign) and increased money
supply (inflation tax). Internal debt was largely monetized, contributing to a sharp rise in prices, while, after the war, foreign debt was a
source of long negotiations and international tensions that did not help
to return to international financial stability and, for a few years, made
it difficult for Italy to access the main financial markets, in particular
those in New York.

The transition from war to peacetime exposed the conflict's negative
impact on the economy: excess capacity in various sectors (first and
foremost shipbuilding), inflation and bank crises, all of which contributed to social unrest and the fascist reaction to it. The postwar economy suffered from the burden of large conglomerates, which were
internationally uncompetitive and heavily leveraged with the banking
system, resulting in the collapse of the third largest Italian bank, the
"parent" of the Genoese Ansaldo group. State support was needed for
their survival.

The Great War was the watershed between an increasingly integrated world and an epoch of "economic nationalism," protectionism
and trade wars. For Italy, the shock was particularly hard: the replacement of liberal democracy, although very imperfect but in evolution,
with dictatorship. A "culture crisis" spread to every area of Italy's
public life, eroding the credibility of the parliamentary institution.
The subversive Right and the revolutionary Left differed on the
methods for dealing with liberal democracy, not on the need for its
liquidation. Mussolini claimed "Parliamentary cretinism." For thousands of young Italians who had gone through the experience of the
trenches, politics, as interpreted by the liberal elite, became "the great
totem to be demolished."

The catch-up period of the Italian economy, still backward compared to the more advanced ones, continued in the 1920s. Progress

stopped but did not reverse in the following decade. Over the entire 1914–1939 period, therefore, Italy's GDP convergence to the more developed countries slowed down but did not altogether stop. In 1913, the per capita income of Italy was still 52 percent of the British one (73, 70 and 48 percent, respectively, of that of France, Germany and the United States). In 1939, the best prewar year for its economy, Italy had gained a few convergence points with respect to the United Kingdom and the United States. Moreover, it kept its distance from France and lost a little ground only to Germany, where the Nazi regime proved to be economically more efficient that the fascist one.

The end of WWI was followed by inflation, a relatively short but deep GDP contraction, and banking crises (Feinstein 1995). Two large credit institutions wound up in a state of insolvency. The Banca Italiana di Sconto was left to its fate, while Banco di Roma was bailed out but required support for many years to come.

From the end of 1921, Italy's GDP began to grow robustly. The first coalition government led by Mussolini, with the economist Alberto de' Stefani at the Treasury, tried to resume the trend of successful prewar macroeconomic policy. Between 1921 and 1926, domestic public debt fell from 80 to 50 percent of GDP (Francese and Pace 2008: 21). Higher price inflation than in many other European countries prevented the stabilization of the exchange rate and therefore the return to prewar capital and remittance flows. Exports, however, only momentarily benefited from the devaluation of the lira. Overall, in the "liberal" period of the fascist era, between 1922 and 1925, the Italian GDP grew by a good 6.1 percent a year, faster than that of Britain and Germany. Political stability, the suppression of social conflicts and an orthodox fiscal policy seemingly reduced investors' uncertainty. Even relevant liberal personalities, who later became ardent anti-fascists, felt that Mussolini could be tolerated for a short period of time as long as he delivered social peace and fiscal equilibrium. History showed that even people of high moral and intellectual standing can be bitterly mistaken.

Between 1926 and 1930, GDP growth slowed to a modest 2.5 percent per year, almost entirely due to misguided economic policies. In January 1925, Mussolini sanctioned the beginning of the full-blown dictatorship and with it a radical change in economic policy. De' Stefani was replaced at the Treasury with entrepreneur and financier Giuseppe Volpi who, without considering the advantages for Italian exporting sectors with a high labor content such as textiles, agri-food and light mechanics, hastened to reintroduce the import duty on wheat and enact protective measures for the industrial sectors (steel, heavy machinery, chemicals), which had no comparative advantage and were produced only for the internal market. At the same time Mussolini, for reasons of misconstrued national prestige, embarked on a policy of revaluation of the lira which led, in 1927, to the reintroduction of the gold convertibility of the lira at the exchange rate of 92 lire per pound, while both domestic and international experts reckoned that the correct exchange rate was 120. The stabilization of the exchange rate favored the return of foreign capital, even if New York and London bankers argued that an exchange rate between 110 and 120 would have been more stable. The overvalued lira compounded protectionism, freezing Italian exports (Toniolo 1980). Keynes wrote "the lira does not listen even to a dictator and cannot be given castor oil" (Keynes 1923: 113). Unfortunately, once endowed with full dictatorial power, Mussolini showed that those powers could be used to sacrifice the interest of the country to see his grandeur reflected in the currency mirror.

In most countries, inadequate economic policies made the "Great Depression" of the 1930s more severe than it could have been otherwise. Italy was not an exception. Policy mistakes were particularly damaging given the relative weakness of the economy. The international context did not help. There is broad scholarly consensus that the crisis could have been mitigated by monetary and fiscal policy coordination among the main countries, such as to avoid monetary wars (namely competitive devaluations), tariff hikes and strict controls on capital movements. Difficult international relations, the poisoned fruit of the Versailles "truce" that ended the WWI and the absence of effective multilateral economic organizations made such coordination unthinkable. Each country followed its own idiosyncratic policies. In 1931, when London abandoned the convertibility of the pound, Mussolini did not even consider a realignment of the lira to the new sterling exchange rate. Consequently, Italy entered the Great Depression with an overvalued currency. The "strong lira" was an entirely political decision, dictated by misconceived reasons of prestige. The attempt to keep the exchange rate fixed at the level established in 1927 required interest rates to stay high, with a negative impact on investment. GDP fell by about 6 percent in 1930 alone. Substantial amounts of foreign exchange reserves were committed to supporting the lira. When the reserves dangerously dwindled, controls on capital export were introduced. The gold convertibility of the lira, sanctioned in 1933 also by participation in the "gold block" led by France, became a mere fiction. The gold convertibility of the currency was de facto suspended, while the propaganda continued to magnify the strength of the lira.[6]

Public spending increased, but not enough to boost aggregate demand. In 1934, GDP returned to the level of 1929, thanks in part to spending in preparation for the military adventure in Abyssinia. The sanctions of the League of Nations followed, to which the regime responded by officially launching an autarchic plan, not without involuntarily humorous aspects. Autarchy was a huge mistake for a manufacturing economy that was poor in raw materials. Between 1934 and 1939, however, GDP increased by about 4 percent per year, more than that of France and the United States, which had belatedly adopted expansionary policies, but Italy grew less than the United Kingdom and Germany, both aggressively responding to the crisis, although in different ways and at very different periods.

Around the 1930s, spurned by the crisis, fascism brought about a second wave of *southernization* of the public administration. Mussolini was aware of what was called the "employomania" of the South; he also knew that without a state outlet, the intellectual layers of the left-behind regions could become a fearsome opposition force. Consequently, he favored the absorption of young workers from Naples and Palermo, no matter if they had the requisites or could proficiently work. What was also disregarded was that the new bureaucrats brought localist cultures and untransparent procedures that became common to Italy's public administration.

The resulting loss of human capital was burdensome for the South, particularly given the feeble starting conditions. Fascism was also interested in combating a competing anti-state power like the Mafia but did nothing to improve the level of social capital. Large swathes of the population remained completely marginalized. The situation in the most remote villages of the South during the fascist regime is well pictured in Carlo Levi's novel *Cristo si è fermato a Eboli*.[7] A medical doctor and painter, exiled for his anti-fascist activity by the Special Court for the Defense of the State, Levi was sent to Gagliano, a village in the Southern Basilicata Region plagued by miserable living conditions and malaria, where only a few people could live decently: the Fascist Party delegate, two doctors nicknamed "donkey-curers" by their patients, the priest and the pharmacist. Levi encounters a local primitive culture, imbued with magical thinking. Love filters and mysterious plots crowd a language and an imagined reality that tries to overcome hopelessness. Under the earth, villagers suspect the existence of immense buried treasuries that one day will be revealed; above the earth, the state is the enemy, bringing only a few jobs and meaningless wars that even make young men mutilate themselves rather than leave for the battlefields. For the Basilicata people, notes Levi, "Rome is nothing, the rich people's capital, the center of a foreign and malign state." In Gagliano everybody feels close to the brigands, whose violent deeds are narrated on cold evenings by the fireplace as heroic acts of rebellion.

Features of the economic structures under the fascist regime for decades remained ingrained in Italy's economic life. While before 1914 competitive markets were praised as a means to achieve efficiency, under fascism corporatism gave way to producers' collusion that was purported and professed by the regime. The word "competition" acquired a negative connotation in the press (Gigliobianco and Giorgiantonio 2017). Monopolies and cartels were not only tolerated but often favored, as was common practice in Continental Europe. Although interlocking practices between private and public interests were common before the war, industrial policy became a priority of the fascist dictatorship. The market economy was not replaced with a "planned" economic policy of the Nazi type. However, an anti-free market mentality consolidated over time. Nonetheless, some technological trajectories that had begun before WWI were fully exploited by the Italian industry in the postwar period. Cheap hydroelectric energy made possible the introduction of various innovative processes such as the production of high-quality steel from scrap iron, aluminum from bauxite and fertilizers from acetylene. In the 1920s, foreign direct investments played a significant role as technology drivers, but domestic innovation was also quite lively. Snia Viscosa became the second largest world producer of rayon (or artificial silk, as it was then called), a typical mass consumption good. Although in later years protectionism and controls on capital movements reduced the flow of foreign direct investment, it would be wrong to picture Italy under fascism as a technologically stagnant economy and society. The import of foreign technology continued through foreigners' patenting, licenses and joint ventures. During the post-1935 autarky, the government favored and promoted "the establishment of laboratories and research facilities, particularly in the chemical and rubber companies such as Montecatini, Snia and Pirelli. Developing new technologies was considered a matter of national interest." With respect to the United States and Germany, however, technological advances suffered from the weak connection between science and industry. (Barbiellini et al. 2013: 383).

The intrusive role of the state created privileged links between politics and individual entrepreneurs, who duly applied for party membership. A huge web of relations, controls and allowances, based on the powers of the public administration and increasingly subordinated to the National Fascist Party, created a substratum of bureaucratic and judicial powers that remained in the following decades, sometimes strengthening its own power. Independent labor unions were suppressed and replaced with fascist-controlled organizations. All forms of dissent were suffocated. As in the case of Carlo Levi, thousands of dissidents were either sent to internal exile or forced to emigrate. The control of the press, already in the claws of business interests, became totalitarian. After 1938, barbaric legislation deprived citizens of Jewish origin of such basic rights as attending public schools, holding public sector jobs, owning land and bank equity (Pavan 2004).

Workers gave up their right to protest, trading it for welfare assistance provided by the state: housing, post-labor recreational activities and job placement, all contingent on joining the Fascist Party. The agricultural policy was centered around the "battle for wheat," irrationally aiming at making the country self-sufficient in grain production, for which it had no comparative advantage outside the Po valley and limited areas in the South. Nonetheless, images of Mussolini, il Duce bare-chested digging the land pleased the masses, even though the economic and welfare conditions of most people did not improve. Per capita private savings ratios never returned to pre-1913 levels, absolute poverty incidence did not continue its prewar downward trend, nor did income inequality as measured by the Gini coefficient, as already mentioned, and the per capita income gap between the country's Center–North and South widened, particularly in the 1930s (Vecchi 2017).

Policymaking during the Great Depression was not a sequence of errors only. If, as already noted, Mussolini's veto of a realignment of the lira to the new parity of the pound made an effective macroeconomic policy impossible, a major looming banking crisis was successfully prevented. At the end of 1930, the large Italian universal investment banks, holding in their portfolios over 50 percent of the shares in the largest listed companies, were not only illiquid but also insolvent. They turned to the government for help. There was an imminent danger of a banking crisis such as the one that, months later, would destroy the German and Austrian major banks and the industrial companies connected to them, plunging those countries into the most severe banking crisis in their history. A quick and secret intervention by the government spared Italy from a similar fate. The rescue operation was secretly planned and executed entirely outside the public administration. Mussolini put it in the hands of a trusted financier, Alberto Beneduce, a former socialist and not a member of the Fascist Party. The industrial portfolio of the banks was taken over by state-controlled entities and transferred, in 1933, to the Institute for Industrial Reconstruction (IRI), giving rise to a huge public holding, operating, however, under the Civil and Commercial Codes, with no interference from the public administration. IRI controlled manufacturing, transport and electrical companies, as well as the banks that it had bailed out with a robust injection of liquidity as partial compensation for giving to IRI their industrial portfolio and committing to transforming themselves into commercial banks. Those new institutes operated in the short-term credit market, from which the 1936 banking law precluded long-term investments that were reserved for specialized institutions. The rapid and effective intervention prevented a very serious liquidity crisis and, between 1931 and 1934, minimized the potentially extremely high costs for the real economy (Toniolo 1980, 1995). We will see that, after the WWII, IRI played an important role in the reconstruction and the post-1950 economic development.

Italy entered the World War II economically and militarily tired after five years of fighting in Ethiopia and Spain, as well as completely unprepared. The economy somehow held up until 1943, with GDP declining by "only" 22 percent from the beginning of the war, only to collapse in the following two years. Until 1942, inflation was kept somewhat under control, but it exploded afterward. After accepting unconditional surrender in 1943, Italy was occupied by Allied and German forces, fiercely fighting for every inch of land.

At the end of the conflict and of the partisan resistance, in April 1945, almost half a million Italians were dead or missing. The economy was in shambles, foreign trade had been reduced to nothing and GDP – 44 percent lower than six years earlier – had fallen back to the 1905–1906 level. The economic efforts of an entire generation had been wiped out. One in four workers had lost his or her job. Masses were starving. Some food and medical aid was provided by the Allied liberation forces that only a few months earlier had been pictured as invaders. Rules of civic coexistence were no longer kept in large parts of the country which were enduring rampant destruction, robberies, revenge and desperation.

3.3 Setting the Stage: Reconstruction

Italy regained full sovereignty in 1946. In the same year a majority of the electors, for the first time including women, voted to end the monarchical regime and transform Italy into a republic. By 1949, GDP had already overcome the level of 1939, the best prewar year. In the four immediate postwar years, Italy's GDP grew by an average of 15.8 percent per year. This extraordinary episode, now mostly forgotten, was one of the few moments in Italian history when political parties and civil society displayed cohesion and determination in reacting to situations that were – euphemistically speaking – difficult.

The success of the reconstruction depended on numerous factors, domestic and international. Some authors note that the weariness of war and of ideological conflicts fueled a widespread pragmatic desire to clean the slate. However, simplistic notions such as the need for safety and craving for normality do not do justice to a much more complex evolution (Stone 2013: 5). Already in 1944, the Stevenson report, delivered to the US Administration, highlighted the friendly attitude manifested toward the Allies by large swathes of the Italian population. In 1945, US General Mark Clark acknowledged the contribution to the US Army offered during the war by Italian "soldiers, partisans and civilians." Americans of Italian origin in the US positively influenced the Administration's attitude toward the country, also due to the fear that, left to itself, Italy, like Greece, could wind up under new chaotic or dictatorial regimes. The benevolent attitude of the

United States, and to some extent of the Soviet Union, opposed the harsher British stance and spared Italy the long Allied occupation that existed in Germany and Japan. It has been argued (Boltho 2013), however, that this turned out to be a mixed blessing. It was certainly good for Italians to soon become masters again of their own house and democratically draft their new constitution, rather than having it somehow 'dictated' by an occupying power as in the case of Japan. However, the downside of the postwar Italian settlement was that there was a smaller degree of institutional continuity than in the Japanese case.

Crucial to the relatively smooth transition from dictatorship to democracy was the acceptance by the strong Italian Communist Party of Western democratic rules, as well as its participation in the first postwar governments, in a climate of cooperation between opposing ideologies that inspired the Republican Constitution. Trade union moderation allowed the postwar reconstruction to take place in an environment of relative social peace. In 1946 inflation was close to spiraling into hardly controllable expectations. It was blocked in 1947 through a much-criticized but effective credit crunch implemented by two governors of the Bank of Italy, Luigi Einaudi and Donato Menichella. In the meantime, however, inflation greatly reduced the real value of the public debt accumulated during the war. Consequently, the Italian Republic was born with a debt-to-GDP ratio of only 32 percent, the lowest in its unitary history.

The international framework was decisive in the context of a "postwar settlement" that took a very different path from that of 1919 (Judt 2010). Italy's first postwar head of government, Alcide De Gasperi, was aware of the potential danger arising from the ideological confrontation between supporters of a system based on parliamentary democracy and those in favor of Marxist collectivism. He decided to support Italy's adhesion to the international monetary institutions, also as an "external constraint" to domestic policies, binding Italy to the West, even in case the Communist Party were to prevail. The strong role of the state in directly managing the economy was one of the cornerstones of the doctrinal elaborations of the anti-fascist parties, both of Marxist derivation and of Catholic origin. The constituents' priority was to prevent the future return of fascism, but they were also wary of the experience of liberal pre-fascist Italy. Consequentially, the constitutional debate converged on two priorities: The first was avoiding a return to the liberal-era government, connotated by the fragility of parliamentary majorities and the weak powers of the heads of government; the second priority went in the opposite direction, dreading the ease with which fascism had increased the powers of the executive, which allegedly opened the way to the totalitarian regime. Deeply uncertain about the future electoral outcomes, the constituents converged on safeguarding as much as possible the democratic order, at the cost of sacrificing the efficiency of a stable executive. In the following four decades, this configuration would display a continuous rotation of governments, counterbalanced by surprising stability of parliamentary majorities. This naturally led to conferring a broad centrality to the parliament, with respect to the other constitutional authorities. The political parties' role went much beyond that of mediators between the state and the people, acquiring a more encompassing aspect than in other democracies.

As already mentioned, since it was associated with the pre-fascist era, liberalism was looked upon with suspicion. However, Einaudi and De Gasperi promoted a more open market economy and aligned Italy's politics with the European partners in the construction of a more integrated area. At the same time, they firmly adhered to Atlantic cooperation. In 1947, De Gasperi's official journey to Washington determined the end of the large coalition of all the anti-fascist parties and the formation of a government excluding the communists. De Gasperi's turnaround was important in institutional terms because it determined the end of the "assembly governments," encompassing all the non-fascist parliamentary parties and it was favored by the communists as a direct and unique expression of popular sovereignty. The end of the large coalition marked instead the birth of partisan dialectics within the Italian Parliament. In the 1948 elections, the communist alternative was defeated, defusing the risk of popular uprisings. A long period of odd stability began: A multitude of governments led by exponents of one single party, the centrist Christian Democracy, retained control of most of the political power without a real alternative.

The relationship between Italy and the United States had important political and financial consequences that were engineered in the first years of the Republic. It is difficult to quantify the contribution to Italy's reconstruction of the billion and a half dollars that the Marshall Plan allocated to Italy between 1948 and 1951. The funds arrived when the reconstruction was at an advanced stage, averaging about 2 percent of

GDP, less than the 2.5 percent obtained on average by European countries (Eichengreen and Uzan 1992). Nonetheless, it played an important role "in the distribution of the costs of stabilization, in supporting the modernization of industrial plants" (Crafts and Magnani 2013: 77) and in providing the much-needed foreign currency for the import of raw materials. Even more important were the institutional consequences of the Marshall Plan. While the war wounds were still bleeding, the plan forced European governments to sit around a table in Paris to coordinate the use of American aid, as part of a new cooperative institution, at the OEEC (the future OECD). The dollars of the plan also allowed for the functioning of the European Payments Union, a now forgotten institution, crucial in initiating the transition from the system of international payments on a bilateral basis, so much detrimental to world trade in the 1930s, to a multilateral system[8]. It opened the way to full convertibility of the currencies achieved in 1959. In 1947, Italy joined the International Monetary Fund, borrowing the dollars needed to subscribe to its quota. The reconstruction, therefore, did not consist only of the restoration of infrastructures and plants; it was also a creative moment for institutions, political practices, intermediate organizations (first of all the large trade unions) and an international opening that overturned the fascist economy of the 1930s.

Industrialists were largely inclined to pick up the corporatist legacy of fascism and side with radical trade unions to request tariff protection from international competition. If that was the case, the political leadership was able to overcome its long-standing protectionist instincts, betting on the fruits of a slow but steady drive toward ever-increasing international competition. This imperceptible outcome had two positive effects. On the one hand, the opening of the economy and the adhesion to international institutions provided for a guarantee – another *vincolo esterno* – against the danger of a communist victory or a fascist revanche, all too present in other southern European countries: Spain, Portugal, Greece, and the Balkans. On the other hand, trade liberalization prevented the quite inefficient and sometimes corrupt public administration from hampering economic life.

3.4 A Golden Age

The years 1951–1972 were the Golden Age of the Italian economy, when GDP grew at an annual average rate of 5.6 percent at constant prices (about 4.8 percent per capita). As a result, over the same period of time, Italy's per capita income jumped from about one-third to two-thirds of the US per capita income. Product per hour worked followed a similar trend, reaching 71 percent of that of the US and overtaking the United Kingdom in 1973. The "total factor productivity," a good indicator of technical progress, grew at rates never recorded in Italy either before or after this Golden Age.

Not only did income increase, but it was less unevenly distributed among people (Vecchi 2017: 314) and between different areas of the country. For the first time since unification, the South grew faster than the national average, narrowing the gap with the Center–North (Felice 2013: 101). The average life span increased from sixty-seven to seventy-two years, reaching the level of the more advanced countries. The poverty rate fell from 34 to 13 percent of the population (Vecchi 2017: 584). These were years in which Italy was less and less seen as a peripheral country, joining, in common perception as well as in international statistics, the countries at the "core" of the world economy.

Needless to say, averages hide differences over time and over economic sectors. The pattern of GDP growth saw a sharp acceleration after 1958, leading, in 1963, to price increases to which the Bank of Italy's monetary policy reacted, or even overreacted, according to some. In the following decade, growth resumed at about the pre-1958 rate. Until 1963, GDP grew faster than private consumption, while capital accumulation proceeded at high speed. For the first time in Italian history, exports of goods and services realized a two-digit expansion: Italian businesses took full advantage of the progressive integration of the country into the international economy. Aggregate demand composition changed after the short 1963 crisis. Private consumption growth outstripped that of GDP, while export and investment growth halved. For the first time since 1945, the expansion of public consumption acquired the leading role in sustaining aggregate demand.

The manufacturing industry was the engine of the Golden Age transformation of the Italian economy. Its production grew on an average by 8.3 percent each year, more than quintupling between 1950 and 1973 (Gomellini and Toniolo 2017: 120). In those same years, agricultural workers (measured as full-time equivalent units) dropped from 43.3 to 16.6 percent of the total labor force. Millions of workers and their families took part in the most colossal internal migration from the countryside to urban conglomerations, and from the South to the North, in Italian history. It is easy to imagine what this meant in terms of social dislocations, human and cultural clashes, and welfare improvement, all accompanied by psychological traumas. Adaptation costs were huge for the likes of the Basilicata peasants described by Carlo Levi (see Section 3.2), who suddenly found themselves living in crowded rooms on the outskirts of Milan. Migrants would work in the booming construction industry, on a seasonal or daily basis not much different from their previous agricultural employments, hoping to sooner or later join their luckier former co-villagers in landing a permanent job with companies like Fiat, Montecatini or Pirelli. Once that was achieved, they would bring their family over and rent tiny apartments. The move of former peasants toward industries had an impact on the urban landscapes as well as on the homogeneity of local communities. Immigrants, often the poorest and least educated Italian citizens, were forced to adjust to alienating lifestyles and climatic conditions and tried to stay close together in closed cultural communities, as their forefathers had done when moving to North Boston, Stuttgart, or Buenos Aires. The consequences of mass immigration on the stronger sense of civic community in the North were so dramatic that they resulted in discrimination, if not outright racism. The social unease would increase in the following decades and would eventually lead to mass discontent, with Northern Italians calling for secession. Later, when the children of the first Southern immigrants were integrated with the North, foreign immigration would again impact social cohesion, this time not only in the northern part of the country.

For those who obtained one, a permanent job in the manufacturing industry meant hitherto unimaginable economic well-being. For the first time in history, the living standards of the Italian masses rose above mere subsistence levels. The postwar Golden Age also saw in Italy the dawn of an "affluent society," as described by John Kenneth Galbraith (1958). In the short span of a generation, the consumer revolution changed the life of Italians just like it had done for North Americans forty years earlier. The fruits of the second industrial revolution were ripe to harvest for the majority of Italian citizens. Households became larger and healthier, with hitherto unavailable access to running water and modern sewage systems. Central heating spread rapidly. Cheap public transport made life easier for commuters.

In Italy's collective memory, the Golden Age stands out for the mass triumph of durable consumer goods. The Vespa scooter and the tiny Fiat 500 became symbols of the dream of private transport available to every citizen come true. They symbolized the realization of individual freedom. Refrigerators, washing machines, televisions and, finally, dishwashers changed the dynamics of domestic work. These appliances liberated women from the burdensome housework they had been confined to for millennia. Not only could they now enjoy their free time away from domestic chores, but they increasingly entered the labor market. Family incomes increased and women's status within the household began to change.

Italy was not the only country, in the thirty years after WWII, to successfully catch up with the more advanced countries. The process was particularly rapid in Germany, already a more advanced country than Italy, and Japan, which had initially been less developed than Italy. The three countries, originally allied during the World War II, came to be known as those who lost the war but won the peace. The Germans spoke of *Wirtschaftswunder*, the Italians of a *Miracolo*, and the French, less dynamically but more patriotically, called this period *"les trente glorieuses."*

Italy's most prominent banker, Raffaele Mattioli, maintained that Italy's development had been by no means "miraculous," being rather the logical consequence of an already existing industrial base; a strong credit ranking by foreign capital investors; the removal of productive bottlenecks in steel or energy; monetary stability; and openness to international trade. Public support was sometimes misplaced but continuous. Finally, the international economic framework was very favorable with many importing countries and a large availability of raw materials.

Mattioli's opinion is beyond dispute: Indeed, there were no inexplicable "miracles." The international framework of the postwar period was much more favorable to economic growth than the period following WWI. The forces that allowed the less advanced countries to develop more rapidly than those at the technological and productive frontier were unfettered from the constraints holding them back between the two world wars: tariff and monetary wars, exasperated nationalisms and economic, political and social dirigisme. The context in which the reconstruction took place created an environment favorable to development and the new "social capability for growth."

Fordism, the dominant technology at the time, was particularly suited to generating development in a country where skilled engineers were available, and the workforce was now free from the scourge of illiteracy. The import and adaptation of US technology to the Italian peculiarities gave surprising and rapid results. The existence of a relatively large domestic market made it possible to exploit economies of scale, especially in the production of durable consumer goods, generating competitive advantages in foreign markets. Direct investments from abroad contributed to the import of advanced technologies, which Italian companies, including small and medium-sized ones, treasured above all with imitation, adaptation and the "reverse engineering."

The new international framework, characterized by the growing openness of international markets, exchange rate stability, orderly flow of capital and growing cooperation between countries, was decisive for freeing the latent social capacity to generate economic development. But the opportunities for growth that opened had to be seized. The "convergence" of Italy toward the more advanced countries was not a mechanical, almost automatic, process. History is not lacking in examples of countries unable to seize the growth opportunities when they arise. Even sailing with favorable tides and winds requires good skippers.

Despite all their limitations, which at the time perhaps seemed greater than they appear today, the political, trade union, economic and professional elites in many cases proved to be up to the task of seizing the opportunities offered by history. A sense of purpose prevailed over the divisions. Very different, even opposing, political and cultural forces converged in the approval of the 1948 Constitution. Coalition governments were formed, leading, even against strong opposing interests, to the opening of international markets and adherence to nascent European institutions. The way the political elite embraced this openness is still significant. Carli even later claimed that by 1953 Italy was probably "the country with the lowest barriers to international trade."[9] Free trade liberalization attained 99.8 percent of agricultural products and 100 percent of raw materials, higher than in all neighboring countries.

Up to 1963, the large supply of low-wage labor available in the countryside and the trade unions' far-sighted behavior allowed wages and productivity growth to be compatible with a sharp increase in investment. The government-owned industrial conglomerate (IRI) inherited from the 1930s was able to produce intermediate goods, such as steel (which since 1887 had always needed customs protection to survive), at competitive prices on the international market. In 1953, a new state-controlled company (ENI) was created to supply oil to the country at the lowest possible price. It grew fast in international markets, competing for drilling concessions in several countries. Its brilliant founder and general manager, Enrico Mattei, died in 1962 when his private jet mysteriously crashed; the causes of the accident have never been ascertained but left a string of suspicions pointing to international competitors. Public finance was kept in equilibrium until the end of the 1960s. The banking and the financial systems remained protected and highly regulated, under the banking law of 1936. In this respect, Italy did not differ much from other European countries in a context of limited international capital mobility. The "financial repression" probably lasted too long, but in the 1950s and 1960s it did not appear to have represented an obstacle to a rather efficient allocation of financial flows.

Yet, mistakes were made also in this favorable context. Electric power companies were nationalized in 1962. It was a requirement by the Socialist Party for its participation in the center-left coalition government with the Christian Democracy and smaller parties of the center, a move somehow akin to Giolitti's political attempts of the first decade of the century to include representation for the working class in the government. From a long-term economic point of view, nationalization was not a good idea. Compensation was paid to the shareholders of the electric power companies, placing a considerable amount of money in the hands of private capitalists who had no investment experience or entrepreneurial capacity in sectors outside their own. In the following years, they took control of large manufacturing companies that did not fare well.

The Gordian knot that was not cut was the one concerning competition policy. While the opening of international markets put the manufacturing industry in a naturally open and competitive market, the sectors with little or no exposure to international competition, especially the services sector, enjoyed natural protection that in the long run reduced their efficiency, thus damaging businesses and also consumers (Cavazzuti 2017, Baldini and Pellegrini 2017).

In 1958, the connection between political parties and economic interests became clearer with the institution of the Ministry for State

Holdings (Ministero delle Partecipazioni Statali). Its official purpose
was to coordinate investment, but a hidden function soon became
apparent: funding political parties. While the association of private
entrepreneurs used to fund its favorite political candidates, public
enterprises were expected to fund all the parties in the government
coalitions.

Italian political reformism faded between the end of the 1950s and
the early 1960s. In March 1962, Budget Minister Ugo La Malfa
presented to parliament a controversial document (called "Additional
Note"), in which he identified three fundamental internal weaknesses
that economic development had not solved: the widening gap between
agriculture and industry; the persistent backwardness of the South
with respect to the North; and a production structure skewed by
distortive private and public consumption behavior. However,
1963 was the year when unemployment fell to its lowest level ever,
and La Malfa's alarm was not followed by political reforms.

Growth acceleration in 1958–1963, marking the zenith of the "economic miracle," reached "almost Japanese" growth rates (GDP
growth peaked in 1961 at an unprecedented 7.8 percent). "Less than
fifteen years after the end of the war, labor markets turned from
structural unemployment to full employment. In fact, one of the peculiarities of the experience of 1950–1963 relative to the long-term trend
was the very rapid growth of labor inputs to the economy. In 1963 the
unemployment rate reached its lowest historical level, 2.6 percent"
(Rossi and Toniolo 1996: 442). In this context, nominal wages
increased by 13 percent in 1962 and by 18 percent in 1963, largely
more than GDP growth. The increase in domestic demand, which
resulted from those wage increases, led to a sharp rise in the rate of
inflation (up to 8 percent at the end of 1963) while creating a deficit in
the current account balance of payments (−1.5 percent of GDP, in
1963). The external deficit increased significantly in the wake of a flight
of capital, triggered by different factors: the concern ahead of the
formation of the first center-left government (December 1963); the
previous year's nationalization of the electric power companies; and
the rumors around the upcoming devaluation of the lira. Price stability,
one of the economic cornerstones of the previous decade, was thus
called into question. The Bank of Italy applied monetary breaks to
domestic demand expansion, reducing GDP growth in 1964 to "only"
3.7 percent. Unemployment rose to 3.8 percent in 1965. Given the

Table 3.1 *Annual average growth of the main macroeconomic variables, 1951–1972 (constant 1963 prices)*

	Gross domestic product	Fixed investments	Exports	Private consumption	Public consumption
1951–1972	5.6	7.1	9.5	4.8	7.0
1951–1958	5.3	9.7	12.0	4.1	4.8
1958–1963	6.7	9.9	13.1	4.8	4.4
1963–1972	5.1	4.1	6.5	5.4	10.3

Source: data from Baffigi et al. (2013)

growth expectations created in the previous years, the central bank was blamed by both entrepreneurial and worker organizations for generating a "recession." In the following years, however, growth resumed roughly at the pre-1958 rate (Table 3.1).

The "crisis" of 1963–1964, though negligible from the macroeconomic point of view, triggered reactions and highlighted weaknesses of the Italian economy and society that would characterize its future development.

Since the end of the war, the Italian industrial development model had been based on the availability of low-paid workers. With full employment in 1962 and 1963 and after several years of labor cost compression, wage demand became impetuous. Weak and unstable governments were unable to manage the ensuing social tensions. The alarm among the Italian entrepreneurs was so acute that the illegal export of capital became a phenomenon of macroeconomic relevance. In 1963, the outflow of banknotes through the mountains of Switzerland or toward Liechtenstein was estimated by the Bank of Italy at 1,470 billion dollars, higher than the negative balance of payments (1,251 billion). The chain of critical factors at play will become a pattern in the following decades: Sociopolitical instability fed into financial instability and the latter had direct repercussion on the growth rate of gross investment in industry, which fell from an average of 9.1 percent between 1951 and 1962 to 3 percent in the period 1963–1970.

Economist and public manager Pasquale Saraceno (1963) acknowledged the revolutionary character of full employment in Italian history by presciently arguing that, henceforth, both business management

and macroeconomic policies would have to innovate to adapt to an age
in which growth would come only from productivity increases. In fact,
firms struggled to meet the demand for high wages and investment at
the same time. The public administration did not adjust to the regulatory and service provision tasks required by a modern market
economy.

The nationalization of the electric power companies in 1963, and
several cases of untransparent exploitation of the financial market,
caused a major credibility blow to the stock market and put an end
to the postwar optimism among investors. The opportunity to transform the nature of the Italian financial system from a bank- to a
market-oriented one was lost. The direct link between households'
savings and production units was severed, and this was unfortunate
because it could have represented a strong propulsor for the Italian
economy. In 1962, stocks amounted to 37 percent of the total securities issued, but only one year later their share declined to only 20
percent. The consequences on the structure of Italy's capitalism would
be significant. Household savings were either kept in banks or invested
in government securities, and bank credit became by far the most
important funding channel for firms.

In those years, endogenous technical progress did not grow fast
enough. Italy had reached a development stage in which the advantages of backwardness, such as the abundance of cheap labor and
imported technology, began to yield fewer benefits. In the 1960s, the
flows of new migrants slowed down, and the labor market tightened.
The labor–capital conflict that fascism had suppressed and the contempt that industrialists had earned for their compromises accommo-
dating the fascist regime exploded in a new season of conflictual
labor relations.

The long-term effect was that the private investment rate slowed
down and remained low. Large private firms, Fiat, Pirelli and Falck,
were in the hands of the families that founded them, forming an
unaccountable oligarchy (some firms kept secret even their turnout
until 1974) that resembled even aesthetically that of the old medieval
princes. Three changes in the behavior of private entrepreneurs had
long-term consequences: (a) the already-mentioned loss of credibility
of the stock market, which caused a retrenchment of risk capital and
the preference of most issuers for corporate bonds, bank credit and
non-contestable private ownership; (b) the flight of savings from the

country, mostly to Switzerland, often in parallel with tax evasion and fake accounts; (c) the flight from economic activities requiring long-term immobilization of capital. Chemical industries were transferred to the state; the energy sector was nationalized; and Olivetti, the most promising IT company, started to decline in the mid-1960s. The preference for nimble and small-scale activities has characterized Italian capitalism ever since. Interestingly, economic short-termism became more palpable with the crumbling of what Germans define as *Rahmenbedingungen*, framework conditions – an economic environment primarily based on long-term monetary stability that grants certainty of low and stable levels of interest rates, which in turn make it possible to reliably estimate the potential yields of non-financial long-term investments. It is legitimate to infer that, starting with the 1960s, Italy's political short-termism began to produce economic short-termism. The latter, however, morphed also into a myriad of very agile small and medium private enterprises.

For the larger private and public firms, indebtment became the privileged way to grow. In 1971, total debt came short of 50 percent of the firms' assets, or four times the level of their own capital. The State had the same inclination to increase its debt. The convergence of interests of private firms and the public sector had a role in their tolerance for high inflation levels in the seventies and eighties.

The fact that the state assumed responsibility for large-sized productions – chemical, steel or energy groups – was not bad per se. Unfortunately, however, the new generation of public managers who took over state-owned enterprises was a far cry from the outstanding quality of their predecessors. Dubbed "*razza padrona*," this "domineering breed" was more responsive to the agenda of their political referents than to business rationale. After a successful postwar period, IRI and ENI "were increasingly used to smooth social tensions."[10] In 1957, investments and subsidies to the *Mezzogiorno* were boosted, as the situation in Southern Italy had become a major European problem, met by the creation of the Bank for European Investments. The new public managers controlled great industrial plants established mostly in the Southern regions, such as the Finsider steelmaking factories in Taranto and Bagnoli. The financial results in those critical sectors were often ruinous and the impact on the developments of the surrounding regions disappointing. The new high capital-intensive plants did not generate enough local productive activities around them. Often public conglomerates were used by the governing parties to absorb private firms that had gone broken, preventing layoffs and other social consequences. In aggregate, every year in the two decades after 1968, state-owned firms never reached a profit.

For all the complicated circumstances that characterized Italy's business and political environment, the country continued its race toward economic and civil progress in the coexistence of statism in some sectors and the lack of rule enforcement in many private activities. Capital flight, the black economy, tax elusion and unregistered jobs were generally tolerated as minor problems as long as the economy was growing. Private companies increased productivity margins largely by improving labor force organization, increasing work hours, extending overtime and introducing incentives. Reorganization was sometimes enforced with a certain degree of brutality by managers hard-pressed to increase productivity. A season of labor protest began in the 1960s, for various reasons: from political antagonism in Genoa in 1960 to violent outbursts by migrant workers in 1962 in Turin, and finally in a nationwide organized labor conflict at the end of the decade. Growing social turmoil was one of the reasons why an increasing number of entrepreneurs found it expedient to keep firms small; other reasons being the avoidance of national contractual agreements and fiscal visibility. Eventually, however, the vitality of the new breed of entrepreneurs proved surprisingly stronger than it was first expected (Carli 1996:163).

Unfortunately, political parties were slow to embrace dynamism and take responsibility for the evolution of Italian society and economy. Conventionally, the beginning of the 1960s is seen as the time when the political class lost sense of its responsibility. While in 1959, at the Bad Godesberg's conference the German Social Democratic Party inaugurated a cultural season coherent with liberal democracy, the Italian Communist Party delayed its official commitment to the market economy, even though it not only accepted but endorsed free market behavior in the cities, such as Bologna, where its representatives were elected to govern. On the other hand, while the German Christian Democratic Union, after the first decade of fiscal populism, espoused a political culture founded on economic long-term stability, moderate wage increases and balanced public finance, Italy's Christian Democracy became a catch-all party representing diverging micro-interests. Carli saw the difference between Italy and Germany as "a cultural flaw causing an inferiority complex" in Italians, one that transformed the country's successful initial openness to international competition into fearful "internal protectionism" that saw competition in the naturally sheltered service sector as detrimental to the national economy.[11] Domestic market protection created a network of connivance that was overlooked and at times exploited by the political parties. A further difference with Germany was noticed by Einaudi, who lamented Italy's abandonment of what he called "the framework laws" (leggi di cornice), which clearly recalled the "framework conditions" (Rahmenbedingungen) for the stability of monetary and fiscal policy and which – as explained above – had inspired Germany's postwar reconstruction.

The main political party, the Christian Democratic Party, the pivot of all Italian executives from 1945 to 1992, while internally fragmented into various currents from the right-wing nostalgic of fascism to left-wing catholics, remained firmly anchored to society. This bond was both the constant source of its electoral consensus and the reason for its lack of dynamism. An informal contract was established between the party and its electors compensating for political instability through policy immobilism as if a majority of the citizens asked not to be disturbed by confounding public powers, a form of cynicism that was well epitomized by the personality of the party's main leader Giulio Andreotti.

Against this backdrop, the risk of an authoritarian response took shape that could have led Italy to become a dictatorship like Spain, Portugal and Greece. In 1964, a planned coup by generals was uncovered. The following year, groups close to the Defence General Staff discussed an armed counter-offensive in the face of the communist advance. In 1970, a new coup attempt (the Borghese coup) by armed militias was halted at the very last moment. Shortly before, on December 12, 1969, the season of massacre attacks against civilians, perpetrated by neo-fascists began with the bomb in the centre of Milan in Piazza Fontana. Twenty-five years after the end of fascism, political confrontation between Left and Right resumed extremely conflictual tones.

Already at the end of the 1960s, it was clear that Italy would have to adapt its institutions, bureaucracy, financial markets, education, research and the economic role of the state to the characteristics of an increasingly less backward economy (Rossi and Toniolo 1996).

A significant rise in real wages gave an increasing number of people a sense of material inclusion, of participation in the common good. However, the coming of strong unionized workers' organizations scared the entrepreneurs. In 1968–1969, the so-called hot autumn (*autunno caldo*) highlighted a level of labor conflict not seen since the immediate post-WWI years. Strikes, called at the shortest notice and with no warning could disrupt entire industrial sectors. Managers were deprived of their monocratic control over the whole production process. In 1970, the manufacturing industry had to acknowledge wage increases by 24 percent, three or four times higher than productivity growth.

In October 1969, one month after becoming German Chancellor, Social Democrat Willy Brandt managed to convince the trade unions that a revaluation of the currency was good for workers and the whole country. From then onward, German trade union leaders shared with the government the income policy that kept wages and prices aligned with productivity growth. On that occasion, the lira was also a candidate for revaluation, but no agreement could be made between Italy's government and workers' organizations. In the following years, when the international monetary system collapsed, the divergent paths in income policies between Germany and Italy became a reason for the lack of monetary cooperation between the two countries.

Up to the late 1960s, Italy had been, with Germany, the European country with the lowest level of inflation. The robust wage increases that followed the *autunno caldo* did not satisfy the requests of workers and political and trade union representatives. Entrepreneurs responded to higher labor costs by continuous work restructuring in the industrial plants. The working pace became hard to accept particularly for the young workers who had recently immigrated from the South. They were young, with poor education or qualification, with aspirations and life experience that clashed with the management system known as Taylorism. Rage and rebellion were channeled, sometimes violently, in the requests by trade unions that purported the idea of an economic system in which wages, as trade union leader Pierre Carniti said, had to be seen as the "independent variable" from which all the rest descended. Even the largest private enterprises yielded to the pressure, the first one being Pirelli.

In 1969, the distortion between the country's economic strength and its political weakness produced a paradox: Production was so competitive that it created large trade surpluses but, at the same time, the flight of capital was taking about $200million per month out of the country. The paradox lacked any economic logic, but it was a symptom of the yawning credibility gap that the citizens were developing with respect to their state.

Around twenty years after the birth of the Republic, the reformist spirit that in the early 1960s had animated the first center-left coalition definitively yielded, caught between a rock and a hard place. On the one side there was the Communist Party and the trade union Left that saw the industrial conflict as the lever for gaining a stronger position in the political game; on the other side there was the Christian Democracy that wanted to use public spending in order "to feed a growing labyrinth of indiscriminate social interests" (Craveri 2016: 102) by gaining control of the main public expenditure centers. Politics folded into an anomalous formula of statism and civil society laissez-faire, giving free rein to the citizens' instincts and vitalism while public actors controlled powerful economic leverages, inaugurating a hard-to-die method of stabilizing consensus through public expenditure.

The inappropriate use of public spending to oil social tensions would become ever more of a standard practice in the 1970s and, even more so, in the 1980s.[12] It is central to our interpretation of the growth and decline in the Italian economy. In the late 1960s, it was also a consequence of political instability. Governments on average lasted less than one year. Reforms that would have been politically costly were regularly postponed under the constant and real threat of snap elections. The times were strongly connotated by the upper middle class fear, real or expedient, of extremist popular movements eager to upturn the capitalist system. In this respect, the beginning of the 1960s visibly signaled a pattern that would become of paramount importance in the following decades: political uncertainty, social instability, lack of reliable long-term political commitment, a mix that would produce a vicious circle of uncertainty, feeding financial instability that in turn would lower the propensity to invest.

3.5 Growth Slows Down, Convergence Continues, 1973–1991

In the early 1970s, productivity growth slowed in all advanced countries. The fixed exchange rate system created at Bretton Woods in 1944 ended in 1971 with the suspension of the dollar gold convertibility. The Arab-Israeli war of October 1973, known as the Yom Kippur War, compacted the Middle Eastern oil-producing countries, cementing their cartel (OPEC), which in a few months managed to quadruple the prices of the so-called black gold. The already ongoing trend of increasing the price of several raw materials necessary to European, US and Asian manufacturing companies also accelerated.

In Italy, the thrust of the national and domestic growth factors that had generated the high postwar development slowed down and the postwar Golden Age gave way to a Silver Age of economic growth. Between 1973 and 1992, real GDP grew at an annual average rate of 2.7 percent, about half as much as in the previous twenty-three years, but still quite a respectable rate in an international perspective, as growth slowdown was the general economic experience in Europe and the United States. In the 1970s, Italy's total factor productivity growth was faster than in any other European country, while in the 1980s it was second only to that of France. In 1973–1989, the growth of the Italian output per capita was higher than that of any other European country and the United States (Crafts and Toniolo 1996: 10, 16). Across countries, growth rate differences, however, were smaller than in the previous two decades when most of the convergence process had been realized. Italy's catch-up with the most advanced countries continued, although at a much more moderate speed. In 1995, Italy's gross product per inhabitant reached 71 percent of that of the United States, 98 percent of that of the United Kingdom and 89 percent of that of West Germany (Table 1.3). Output per hour worked (labor productivity) registered a greater convergence (Fig. 3.1).

The 1973–1993 growth rate was the average result of developments in three different periods of time. Between 1973 and 1978, GDP grew at a quite respectable yearly average of 3.5 percent, even in 1975 during the first postwar recession with a 2.1 percent GDP loss. The economy considerably slowed down in 1978–1983, with GDP growing by 1.2 percent per annum (we will soon see the reasons for this mediocre performance). In 1984 growth rebounded to an average 2.7 percent in the following eight years.

From economic, social, and political points of view, the 1970s were extremely contradictory years, still subject to contrasting historical analyses reflecting the deep social and ideological fractures of the time, still the subject of very emotional discussions.

GDP per hour worked   Total, US dollars, 1975 – 2021

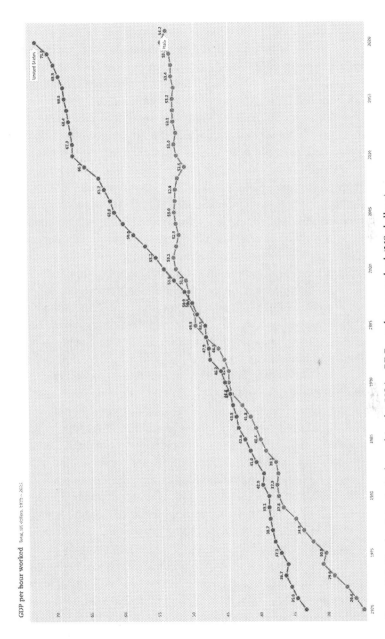

Figure 3.1 Productivity in Italy and in the USA: GDP per hour worked (US dollars)

Source: https://data.oecd.org/lprdty/gdp-per-hour-worked.htm

73

The continuation, albeit at a reduced pace, of the convergence process was also achieved through policies that avoided the implosion of national cohesion, an indispensable element of the "social capability for growth," and supported aggregate demand at the cost, however, of delaying and making less incisive the necessary modernization. Relatively weak political leadership failed to effectively counter the weight of robust "distributive coalitions" (trade unions and business and professional interest groups). In the longer term, as we will see, the costs of the imperfect adjustment of the Italian institutions and production structure to those typical of an economy that is approaching maturity became evident in the 1990s.

The Italian economy broadly followed the evolution of the Western one, from which it could not detach itself, but it did so by "revealing the unpreparedness and inadequacies of our ruling classes, the delays that had accumulated in adapting the institutions for the development of the economy and society, the fractures that crossed the political system and the culture of the country itself" (Salvati 2000: 36). The problems with the political order were more articulate, as we will see later.

The 1973 shock was met with "austerity" measures, often occasional and confusing, such as the obligation to alternate vehicles with even or odd number license plates in order to ration petrol. A long phase of inflation began in all the so-called advanced countries. However, price increases were unusually high and persistent in Italy. Only the United Kingdom recorded price increases similar to Italy's in the 1970s, but the policies of the 1980s brought British inflation back to normal rates, while Italy managed to clear the inflation differential with respect to its main international competitors only in the 1990s when it was one of the stipulations required for joining the euro.

In 1974, public opinion suffered a humiliation caused by the $2bn loans conceded by the Bundesbank only after the sale of Italy's golden reserves. In 1975, Italy experienced the first drop in GDP since the war. The recession was countered by strong expansionary fiscal and monetary policies, ones that were needed also to meet the great demand for wage increases. Low interest rates, the increase in the money supply, the devaluation of the lira against the dollar and the heightening of uncertainty due to the government crisis at the end of the year, all converged in producing a crisis in the balance of payments that forced Italy, in January 1976, to adopt the extraordinary measure of a long

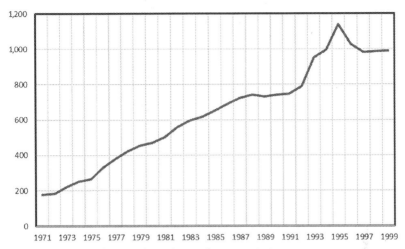

Figure 3.2 Italian lira per deutsche mark 1971–1999
Source of data: Eurostat

closure of the official foreign exchange market (Ciocca 2007: 300). The annual increase in consumer prices, which in 1975 had reached 25 percent, declined only gradually in the following decade.

Italy's monetary response may be appreciated in relation to the German one. Figure 3.2 shows the constant devaluation of the lira vs. the deutsche mark. Starting from the fall of the Bretton Woods agreements, the lira collapsed to one-fifth of its starting value in the twenty-seven years between 1971 and 1998. Devaluations compensated for the external imbalances caused by Italy's economic policies. The frequency of Italy's monetary adjustment impacted the economic structure of the country, making it harder for private entrepreneurs to engage in productions requiring capital immobilization for many years or decades (such as in the chemical or engineering sectors). Long-term financing became more difficult to obtain. Many producers concentrated on nimble activities connotated by short-term or flexible investments, such as the fashion industry. Others adjusted to productions that could take advantage of the price competitiveness favored by the frequent devaluations (Fig. 3.2). The structure of the economic activities reverberated on the demand for labor qualifications.

After the *autunno caldo* of 1969, a series of measures were adopted, often necessary but not included in a long-term organic plan, to extend and improve the welfare state. Business subsidies were also indiscriminately granted. Instead of a new social contract, accommodation became the name of the game. What happened was that political interference in the allocation of resources grew through various forms of subsidized credit that reduced the allocative efficiency of the credit system. Secondary and tertiary school enrollment continued to increase, but the overall quality of the educational system declined (Bertola and Sestito 2013: 255, Vecchi 2017: 202). The time required for civil and administrative justice to deliver a sentence lengthened (Bianco and Napolitano 2013). Public enterprise weakened due to requests for employment support regardless of efficiency criteria. The labor market became more rigid.

Italy specialized in low and medium technology sectors, even if there was a continuous increase in the quality of products in many sectors of traditional Italian manufacturing: "Made in Italy" par excellence (Federico and Wolf 2013, Amatori, Bugamelli and Colli 2013). Production was further concentrated in small and medium-sized companies, more flexible and therefore better able to adapt to an economy that was subject to repeated shocks, but less capable of research and development. It was largely thanks to this flexibility, another ingredient of the "social capability for growth," that Italy was able to maintain its share of world trade.

The lack of political responsibility could be exemplified by the growing level of public expenditure compared to the stability of public revenues (Fig. 3.3). At the beginning of the 1970s, public spending amounted to 35 percent of GDP. In 1975 it was already over 45 percent, while tax revenues remained stable at around 27 percent, about 10 percentage points below GDP compared to France and Germany (Rossi 2007).

Politics accommodated all the requests rather than leading the modernization of society. An overdue labor reform was introduced in those absorbing the zeitgeist of strong revendication. A further exemplification is provided by the retreat of the agricultural workers in the South, where the poverty caused by unemployment was offset by an exponential growth in invalidity pensions, which exceeded those of old age (in 1974, against 625,337 old-age pensions, 1,487,119 invalidity pensions were paid in the special fund for direct farmers) and were intended as a measure for maintaining public order in the South. The idea that democratic stability had to be preserved at any cost became more relevant in the following years when terrorist attacks (often of

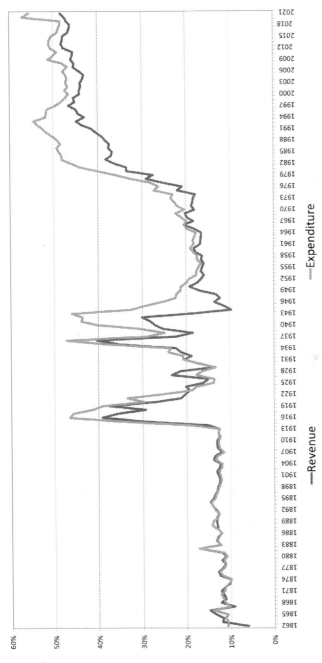

Figure 3.3 General government revenues and expenditures, percentage of GDP (1862–2021)
Sources: Francese et al., (2008), Baffigi (2015), ISTAT (1958), ISTAT (1991), ISTAT (2011), RGS (2011), ISTAT Database, Bank of Italy Statistical Database.

unknown origin) shocked the citizenry and highlighted Italy's fragility in the face of violent forces.

This kind of social contract could remain in place only under the condition of strong economic growth and relatively stable interest rates. In fact, the real policy response was provided by growing inflation, originally triggered by the rise in oil prices and then accentuated by the indexation of wages to consumer prices, in some cases more than proportional, sanctioned by what years later Carli defined as "the unfortunate agreement for the single point of contingency" between Confindustria (the main association of industrialists) and the trade unions (Carli 1993) and what became known as the "*scala mobile*" (escalator) agreement, damning Italy to years of high inflation and exchange rate instability. The whole policy framework became dominated by hidden taxation (inflation) and devaluations with strongly asymmetric effects on society's different layers: employees vs. freelance workers, exporters vs. consumers. In a social milieu that was already deranged by public order issues – kidnapping, robberies, social turmoil, etc. – instability planted the seeds for a diminished sense of community that would further degrade once growth declined, taxes increased and income distribution became problematic.

Blaming politics in this case may be beyond the point. The authors of the agreement on the "*scala mobile*" were three very respected public figures who embodied the crème de la crème of their respective roles: the president of Confindustria Giovanni Agnelli, scion of the family owning Fiat, charismatic trade union boss Luciano Lama and the prime minister at the time, Aldo Moro, a respected Christian Democrat leader who was later kidnapped and assassinated by the Red Brigades. The necessity to assuage the social tension through an agreement that would damage the country's future is a good example of the degree of short-termism that dominated even the best of minds at the time. If in addition to this we consider that Guido Carli, the governor of the Bank of Italy and one of the most admired policymakers of those decades, accompanied the political economy of the time by purchasing government bonds without limits, maintaining that doing otherwise would have resembled "a seditious act," we will understand the degree of either the sociopolitical pressures piled on Italy at the time or of its elites' short-sightedness.

In the meantime, political parties had taken complete control of public decisions often shielded from public scrutiny. The large budget deficits in the public sector resulted, in the 1970s, only in a moderate increase in the debt-to-GDP ratio because the debt was "monetized" thanks to nominal GDP growth rates above the rates of interest whose real value was, in some years, even negative. Debt monetization was made possible, as already mentioned, by a law that obliged the Bank of Italy to buy the government bonds that remained unsold at public auctions in which the government set the price and the market decided how many bonds to buy. To finance the purchase of government bonds, the central bank could only increase the money supply, fueling inflation.

The bad policy choices of the time, in particular the vicious circle of public spending and inflation that characterized macroeconomic policy, can be understood by recalling the climate of extreme social tension. Growing labor tensions met the rebellious culture of revolutionary fringes on the left. Large student mobilizations were confronted by fascists in bloody clashes that marked the large cities' daily lives. The country was under a terrorist wave in what collective memory remembers as the "years of lead," marked by numerous massacres, such as the bombs at Piazza Fontana in Milan (1969), Piazza della Loggia in Brescia (1974) or Bologna's Central Railway Station (1980), and many political assassinations, culminating in the kidnapping and murder of Aldo Moro. The state's murky apparatus has never been entirely exonerated from those criminal acts.

Being on the border of Eastern and Western Europe, Italy was at the center of shadowy international maneuvers in years when Spain, Portugal and Greece were still dictatorships. As already mentioned, in the previous decades, attempted fascist coups d'état and the growing assertiveness of paramilitary associations, sometimes close to politicians nostalgic of the fascist regime, were tolerated by the governments. Hidden masonry lodges generated chains of power that infiltrated the military, the highest public institutions, the judiciary system, the Vatican and the media industry. The discovery of the P2 masonic lodge shed light on the substratum of power connections that had links with foreign dictatorial regimes and infiltrated the highest institutional ranks of the State. The judiciary system and the public administration did not help clear the air and sometimes seemed to engage in diversion maneuvers.

Against the risk of violent social developments, deficit spending and inflation found their political justification in the need to maintain social cohesion and consensus, increasing, albeit in a rather inorganic way, the benefits of the welfare state (Crafts and Magnani 2013).

Although the ability of Italy's economic system to sustain growth and employment in the long term had been weakened and despite the uncertainties caused by the political and social situation, the performance of Italy's economy was surprisingly good. Once more, the dynamics of the economy proved to be resilient. While several entrepreneurs, scared by the social environment, rushed to sell their firms to the state, others, below the radar, were developing new activities mainly outside the larger metropolitan areas. Indulging in historical analogies, one might say that Italy's resilience was another instance of its citizens' attitude toward public powers, reminiscent of previous centuries when they tended to isolate themselves to work vigorously the more they nurtured mistrust in what they perceived as hostile domination at the center of political power. Between 1973 and 1979, the year of the second oil shock, GDP increased by an average of 3.6 percent per year, despite a 1975 decrease. Fiscal and monetary policy supported employment, stimulating domestic demand and business profits. However, the abandonment of fiscal restraint and the strong political intervention in the management of public enterprises and credit made the subsequent necessary macroeconomic adjustment more expensive. The expectations of a continuous rise in prices took root in the behavior of employers and trade unions, particularly when signing collective bargaining agreements that incorporated in advance the price increases expected for the following three years.

The consensus around an anti-inflationary monetary and fiscal policy began to build up in the late 1970s when President Carter appointed Paul Volcker to head the US Federal Reserve System (the central bank). Volcker had the explicit task of taming high inflation, which was growing and apparently intractable so that it even seemed to block any political initiative (Volcker and Harper 2018: 102). It was the signal, reinforced by the appointment of Margaret Thatcher as British Prime Minister in 1980 and the election, in the same year, of Ronald Reagan as US President, that Western countries would consider combating excessive price increases as a primary objective of economic policy. The European Economic Community responded with the creation of a European Monetary System that guaranteed the stability of exchange rates between the currencies of the member countries and, when necessary, "realignments" agreed to avoid competitive devaluations, incompatible with the participation in the European Common Market.

In this new international climate, Italian governments took three decisions of paramount importance to stabilize the economy, reduce inflation and modernize both society and the economy: the participation in the European Monetary System, the introduction of an "income policy" and the abrogation of the rule that obliged the Bank of Italy to purchase the auctioned but un-opted government bonds (the "divorce" between the Treasury and the central bank). Exchange rate stability should have obliged firms to increase productivity rather than prices or face the loss of international competitiveness. The end of automatic financing by the Treasury was intended to induce the policy objective of containing public debt that otherwise would need high interest rates to fund it.

The income policy changed through the political initiatives taken also by socialist leader Bettino Craxi, who called a referendum for the abolition of the "*scala mobile.*" The result was that preventive consultations on wage increases were now made compatible with the reduction of inflation, the maintenance of the real value of wages and an adequate formation of profits to be reinvested. Each of these constraints worked only partially. A radical change in the social conflict had already come after 14 October 1980, when Fiat white collars organized a march through Turin protesting against the major strike that had been called by the trade unions. Unexpectedly, the march gathered 40,000 among workers and private citizens and its success put an end to twenty years of very conflictual labor relations. The new social climate, however, induced the larger firms to recover productivity by cutting jobs.

The trend of the Italian economy in the 1980s followed two distinct phases: The first goes from 1979 to 1983 and the second from 1984 to 1990 (Angeloni and Gaiotti 1990). The first period was characterized by very modest growth in GDP (0.8 percent per year, practically zero per inhabitant). In the second period, development resumed at a rapid pace (3.1 percent as an annual average). Over the period as a whole, the convergence of the average income of Italians with that of the most advanced countries slowed down to zero: By 1990 it had remained constant at around 70 and 100 percent, respectively, in comparison with that of the United States and the United Kingdom, while still growing from 89 to 92 percent compared to Germany. The product per hour process reached 95 percent of that of the United States, surpassing that of the United Kingdom and the Federal Republic of Germany.

The first three years were characterized by a slow reduction of social tensions, a partial restructuring of the industrial system – the first step toward reducing inflation that rose to 20 percent per annum in 1980 – and macroeconomic stabilization. These three elements largely explain the slowdown in the economy, which also coincides with similar trends in all countries engaged in the fight against inflation. The second period, which ended with the 1992–1993 crisis, saw one of the longest expansive cyclical phases of the postwar period in a context of relative social peace and political stability. A new optimism seemed to seize public opinion: Incomes increased and were better distributed while the achievement of well-being comparable to that of Britain was augmented.

The optimism of those years, however, was misleading. The industrial structure was still overly based on medium-level technologies, on companies whose size was too small, often with opaque governance systems, while public enterprises were declining. Above all, however, the opportunity offered by GDP growth was not used to put public finance on a sustainable path in the long term; nor was it possible to contain inflation.

The financial discipline that was expected once the Bank of Italy had been unshackled from the obligation to underwrite government debt did not bear the hoped-for results. The general government budget deficit, which in the 1970s had averaged 7.6 percent of GDP (and, as has been said, largely monetized), was 10.7 percent on average for the following decade. Despite the rising cost of debt, the governments of the 1980s continued their policy of spending beyond the level of fiscal revenues despite the end of the most acute social tensions. As Carlo Azeglio Ciampi said, "the burden of resolving distributional conflicts and finding compensation, rather than a solution, for the losses of the production system has fallen on public budgets" (Bank of Italy 1980: 24). Optimism and consensus were acquired at the cost of leaving the burden of stabilizing public finances for successive governments, making it much more expensive. Despite the growth, the debt-to-GDP ratio of 56 percent in 1970 reached 94 percent by the end of the decade. No developed country had seen such a large increase in debt in such a short period after World War II.

Fiscal and income policy should have contributed in a coordinated way to the reduction of inflation which, according to the Bank of Italy and most economists, did not only have monetary origins (Visco 1995). In particular, the abundant liquidity created by public deficits compromised both the stability of the exchange rate and the control of inflation. The inflation differential forced Italy to agree on numerous devaluations of its currency in the European Monetary System. These were not competitive devaluations, but they intervened *ex post* to recover the lost competitiveness, and the attempt to keep the exchange rate steady was not enough to regulate behavior and avoid excessive price increases.

In this economic policy framework, the reduction in inflation was only a partial success, compared to other countries. For Italy, the 1990s began with strong imbalances on the side of prices and public finance. Italy was also experiencing a sociological context that, although much better off, was as little homogeneous as at the origin of the kingdom, with small-scale industrial or commercial activities prevailing over large-scale economic structures. The number of entrepreneurs was astounding and much higher than in any other industrial country. In this fragmented and more individualistic environment, social tensions were also morphing into something that was at the same time old and new: a general and vigorous sentiment of civic mistrust toward Italy's political order.

Between the seventies and the early nineties, the deficit-to-GDP ratio of the South of Italy stayed well above 25 percent, with a peak of 35 percent, and only in more recent times reached a value of around 15 percent. The North (and in part the Center) had to post substantial primary surpluses to compensate receiving, after the eighties, most of the yields that the state paid on their government bonds. Thus, Italy's public debt caused dependencies and suspicion at the same time. Citizens grew skeptical of the Italian state as a centralized organization presiding over the monopoly of legitimate force, both in its centralized nature and in its force.

Not only did the state's unity appear questionable, torn by the North-vs.-South tensions, but the force itself was doubtful given the burden of the growing public debt. The second category of institutions that constitutes the political order, the respect for the rule of law, seemed gravely underdeveloped in consideration of the virulent spread of organized crime in the Southern regions, the lack of law enforcement in several illegal activities and the judiciary system's general loss of credibility. Finally, the third critical factor in the citizens' trust in the political order, accountability, also seemed insufficient. The political class was not responsive to the interests of society as a whole, while its corruption, self-interest and abuse were clearly visible, fueling widespread popular resentment. At the end of the 1980s, the potential of instability caused by the weakening of Italy's political order was still hidden. It took an unusual combination of crises to make it explode in the 1990s.

4 | *The Trauma of 1992*

4.1 A New World

The Leaning Tower of Pisa is one of the best-known monuments of Italy, and it is a good metaphor for recent Italian history. Ancient, beautiful, precariously inclined, ever close to crumbling, but, lo and behold, still standing. Between 1992 and 1993, about seven centuries after its completion and 500 years after the events mentioned in the first pages of this book, the tower came close to collapsing. The inclination of the monument increased from 3.95° to 4.5° with a sway from the vertical axis of 4.47 meters. The swing was the unintended consequence of the unwise decision to stabilize the building by draining water from under the tower's basement. Seeing the tower close to collapse, the operation was swiftly revoked, and structural interventions, through a system of counterweights, were put in place to bring back the degree of inclination to the previous 1991 width. One could hardly find a better exemplification of what happened to Italy during the same years.

In the early 1990s, Italy's GDP per capita and labor productivity levels were roughly similar to those of Germany, France and the United Kingdom. This remarkable achievement was the result of the secular process of convergence with the initially more advanced European countries. However, in the three previous decades, convergence had slowed down as the "advantages of backwardness" diminished, partially as the result of Italy's success.

The new global context marked by the end of the Cold War proved uniquely challenging for Italy. There are two reasons for that: (a) the factors that had previously sustained catch-up growth, such as the importation and adaptation of foreign technology, became weaker due to the very success of the convergence process; (b) the long-standing, never fully addressed, weaknesses of the Italian economy, institutions and society became more relevant in a historical phase

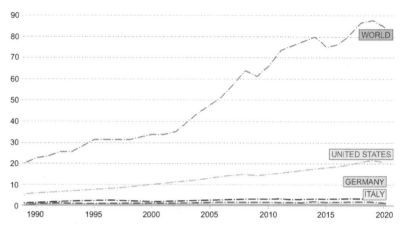

Figure 4.1 Global GDP 1990–2020

Source: https://data.worldbank.org/indicator/NY.GDP.MKTP.CD?contextual=region&
end=2020&locations=IT-1W-DE-US&name_desc=false&start=1989&view=chart

connotated by great dynamism and instability. Both sets of factors had not prevented the previous buoyant growth, even though they had slowed it down after the 1960s, but with the new technology paradigm and in the new context of goods and capital mobility it would have been necessary to move away from the traditional path, based on the import of technology, the transfer of workforce from agriculture to industry and the availability of relatively cheap skilled labor.

On the contrary, the social and political factors behind the slower convergence of the 1980s made it difficult, sometimes impossible, to adapt Italy's economic system to new technologies and international economic relations. Such factors, as we will see, would weigh heavily on the subsequent predicaments of the Italian economy in the changing international economic environment (Fig. 4.1).

The 1980s witnessed the most revolutionary economic event of our time: the end of the economic divergence between the edges of the Eurasian continent, which had characterized the world's economy in the previous five centuries. From the fifteenth century onward, Western Europe had grown faster than China, Asia's major political and economic power. Economic historians note that from the fifteenth to the early nineteenth centuries there was only a "small divergence" as Europe's per capita GDP grew only slightly faster than China's (Broadberry 2016). As a result, around 1800, about "35 percent of the world's land surface was subordinated to Europe" (Findlay and O'Rourke 2007: 144). After 1800, "Modern Economic Growth," for a long time confined to Europe, its overseas offshoots and Japan, resulted in a "great divergence," which can be summarized in just a single number: In 1960, the average per capita income of Western Europe was ten times higher than that of China. For half a millennium, therefore, not only the economy but also the politics, culture, social organization of the so-called West, and even the wars that ravaged it, took place in a framework of ideological "supremacy" based on the technological ability to achieve material well-being that others could not even dream of.

From the end of the 1970s, the economic awakening of China, hitherto a sleeping giant, began to turn the "great divergence" into a "great convergence." China's growth outstripped that of Europe, North America and Japan, the early comers to "Modern Economic Growth." The phenomenon was little noticed in the 1980s and few people understood that the new era of "great convergence" was ushering in a worldwide revolution that would put an end to an era that had lasted half a millennium. At the beginning of the 1990s, the great convergence was strengthened by the economic awakening of India, the other great Asian demographic giant, thanks to the reforms promoted by Finance Minister Manmohan Singh. A world was born in which geopolitics, international trade and the world's distribution of wealth were completely revolutionized.

The end of the semi-millennial "great divergence" was the event that was bound to have, in the long term, the most significant geopolitical, cultural and economic role in designing the "new world." However, at the beginning of the 1990s, other epochal events, concentrated in the short span of three years, accelerated the new world's emergence and gave it a lasting shape. The most significant of these events was certainly the fall of the Berlin Wall, followed by the end of the communist dictatorships in Eastern Europe, the dissolution of the Soviet Union and the German Unification. A large area, accounting for over 10 percent of the world's GDP, emerged from semi-autarchic isolation, which in the case of the USSR had lasted for over seventy years, to participate in the great integration of the international economy (the so-called second globalization). The Cold War, which had characterized the second part of the twentieth century, came to an end. Many restrictions on the transfer of militarily sensitive technologies were lifted, giving a strong impetus to the progress and diffusion of information technology. A microchip-based "general technology" characterized the Third Industrial Revolution, following the steam engine and the electric motor, the general technologies of the two previous industrial revolutions.

On February 7, 1992, in Maastricht – a city at the crossroads of Holland, Germany and Belgium, whose name derives from the Latin "*Traiectum ad Mosam*" (passage to the river Meuse) –the foreign ministers of the European Community signed the European Union Treaty. A horizon of a few years was agreed upon to create the single currency. On December 17 of the same year, the United States, Canada and Mexico signed a free trade agreement, the North American Free Trade Agreement, which subverted a centuries-old tradition of protectionism between the United States and the Latin American country on its southern border.

While these events led to – in a short period – the second globalization, a revolutionary technology, and brought about new economic, political and military international arrangements, Italy was going through a deep crisis, in which the economic shock, albeit intense, was perhaps the least relevant aspect in shaping its successive history.

To grow in the world emerging from the shocks of 1989–1992, the Italian economy required considerable adjustments, first and foremost of a cultural kind, by Italian entrepreneurs, workers, political decision-makers and opinion-makers. As we shall see, Italy's previous "social capability for growth" turned out not to be up to the challenges of the post-1992 decades.

Among the weaknesses that impacted Italy's capacity to adjust to the new technologies, five stand out as particularly crippling: (a) An unprecedented level of political, financial and institutional instability that blurred the perspective of investors in the new sectors; (b) The relatively low average level of education of the population, which little mattered in the previously prevailing Fordist technology environment, requiring only a handful of good engineers, but crucially relevant for the diffusion and adaptation of the information and communication technology; (c) The decrease, particularly from the 1980s onward, in the size, scope and productivity of the large firms, the best positioned to compete internationally in the high-tech sectors and the ablest to invest in research, with positive fallouts and externalities for the small and medium-sized enterprises; (d) A rigid and segmented labor market coupled with a welfare state focused on old-age pension, inefficient in favoring labor mobility through adequate unemployment benefits and retraining, at a time when technology and labor organization required flexible labor markets, while preserving individuals, families and local communities from the consequences of a more dynamic context; (e) An exceptionally high public debt-to-GDP ratio, which as we will see would require drastic fiscal policy changes with an economic as well as a social impact.

4.2 The Many Crises of 1992

It is no exaggeration to define 1992 as a fatal juncture between global transformations and Italian domestic problems. During that year facts and processes that had been slowly maturing in the previous decades coalesced and would result in a traumatic twist in Italy's history with long-term consequences not only on the economy but on Italian society at large.

In the previous pages, we saw that in the 1970s and 1980s governments tried to appease many domestic geographic and social divisions either through monetary policy, leading to high inflation and frequent devaluations, or generous deficit spending, which eventually resulted in high public debt-to-GDP ratios. Lax monetary and fiscal policies contributed to producing feelings of precarity in public life and short-termism in the economy. We also observed how the public debt's instability was one of the main causes of the citizens' long-standing mistrust of public powers, brewing further concerns about the solidity of the state. We stressed that the successive governments' reforming capacity had often been frustrated by staunch ideological confrontation, which leveraged the long-standing social divergences. Moreover, we saw that after the fall of the fascist dictatorship, the power of the executive branch of the government was purposely limited by the republican constitution and, on the contrary, the economic penetration of political parties had grown pervasively through a system of public enterprises. Even against this backdrop, Italians were able to produce a vibrant economy. In a society that is very supportive of the family, and one rich in communitarian rhetoric, private welfare was increasingly at odds with the inefficiency of public institutions. Forms of self-defense (or co-responsibility) from the country's

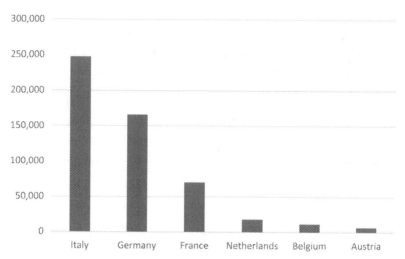

Figure 4.2 Number of lawyers per country
Source: Statista

predicaments gave the Italian economy some of its unique features: the citizens' high propensity for savings, the flights of capital to tax havens, the preference for real estate investment, the small size of enterprises, the underground economy, and the collusion between big business and politics. On the other hand, Italy's society was characterized by a strong and growing quest for improved leadership and justice, by increasingly public contempt of the political establishment, as well as by the strong sense of defense of individual rights, as witnessed by the number of lawyers and civil-law suits per capita, much greater in number than those in other countries (Fig. 4.2).

In this context and against the background of the momentous changes in the postwar international economic and political order, Italy suffered from its idiosyncratic crisis, which turned out to have a lasting impact due to its multidimensional features: judicial, political and economic.

On February 17, 1992, a minor political figure was taken into custody in Milan on bribery accusation. He was the first of a large number of politicians and businesspeople jailed on corruption charges by a self-styled "clean hands" pool of public prosecutors. The neologism *Tangentopoli* (Bribesville) was coined by the media to nickname the investigations and trials in the following months and years. The

Milanese prosecutors were soon followed by their colleagues in nine other cities, including Rome, charging political figures and entrepreneurs with corruption. Most of the largest enterprises, such as Fiat, Olivetti and ENI, were involved. The Milanese "clean hands" pool investigated over 5,000 people, including four former heads of government, among whom was Bettino Craxi, the leading political figure of the 1980s who later died in exile. More than thirty people committed suicide in jail, among them the leader of the third-largest private enterprise, Raul Gardini, and the head of the largest public holding company, Gabriele Cagliari. *Tangentopoli* had large international resonance, including in western countries of long-standing democratic traditions that were increasingly concerned about the fallout of political corruption on democracy.

As for Italy, *Tangentopoli* was mostly interpreted as proof that the country had been more corrupt than most other democracies. Scandals in the corporate sector reinforced this conviction: between 1991 and 1992, Fedit-Federconsorzi, a large firm originated by farming consortia, linking the Christian Democratic Party with the agricultural electorate, went bust, causing bank losses in Italy and abroad, putting Italy's credit standing at risk. In July 1992, EFIM, a state-owned conglomerate with 30,000 employees, feud of the Socialist Party, was liquidated. The default hit foreign banks that were exposed for around 3,500 billion lire and caused the downgrading of Italy's credit rating. The link between Italy's economic predicaments, public debt and the corrupted political parties became obvious to the citizens. Looking at the large discrepancy between "perceived" and "actual" corruption, it was also the sign of a people that for centuries had resented the abuses of the rich and the powerful. Finally, it was a sign that Italy's judiciary system had become more independent from political patronage and more capable of fighting the misuse of public power. Whatever opinion one might have of the actual diffusion of corruption, surely the *Tangentopoli* investigations impacted the endemic mistrust of the state and politics by the public at large, which took a wider collective form and became one of the main elements of Italy's public discourse.

The impact was bound to persist. Thirty years later, measuring the citizens' "perceived corruption," Transparency International still reckoned that 85 percent of Italians believed their country was "corrupt." However, when asked if they had personally experienced corruption in the previous twelve months, Italians' responses were in line with those of the citizens of the other advanced countries.[1] This self-deprecation has become so frequent as to be called the "Botswana syndrome," derived from the fact that, in some international comparisons, Italy implausibly resulted at the levels of the poorest African countries. Italian self-bashing is also likely to result in sometimes implausible international Doing Business rankings of Italy.[2]

The domestic political fallout of the corruption investigations and of the fall of the Soviet Union was enormous. The often-misused adjective "revolutionary" perfectly describes the Italian political events of 1991–1992. The two main parties that governed Italy since 1945, the Christian Democrat and the Socialist, were both dissolved. The main postwar opposition party, the Communist, while only marginally touched by the corruption investigation, was also knocked out primarily as the result of the collapse of the Soviet Union. It was recast under the name of the Democratic Party of the Left. Three-quarters of Italy's electors[3] were utterly disoriented by the disappearance, almost overnight, of the parties they had hitherto supported.

4.3 A Constellation of Uncertainties

After the World War II, episodes of political and economic uncertainty affecting the public at large had arisen mainly from conflicts between labor and capital, or communism and capitalism. The fall of the Berlin Wall ushered in a new season in which uncertainty derived from concerns directly affecting the lives of ordinary people: Will welfare continue to increase? Will savings invested in government bonds remain as safe as before? Will Italy hold on to its place within the European Union? Can people trust the government in all these regards?

Since the mid-1980s, concerns about public debt's sustainability assumed the role played in previous decades by fears that a communist government might expropriate savings and real estate property. Government bonds and bank deposits were the favored asset in which Italian households invested their impressive financial wealth; this increased in the 1980s from 110 to 170 percent of Italy's GDP.[4] Workers invested a large share of their savings in government bonds, as the safest assets alongside post office deposits, also guaranteed by the state. Frequently, savings were aimed at supplementing old-age pensions. The financial wealth of Italian households had increased in parallel with the growth of the public debt, linking the stability of the two variables because of the sizable amount of government bonds resulting from deficit spending to cover social security and old-age risks. The fears about debt sustainability resulted in the government bond yields relative to the European benchmark (the so-called *spread*). The cost of bank loans soared in parallel with the increase of interests paid on government bonds. As a good portion of the government debt was held by the banks, the higher the perceived risk of government bonds increased the higher the risk of banks' portfolios, lowering the propensity to offer credit to risky debtors in the private economy. A critical consequence was that innovative investments, riskier in the short term than others, were crowded out. Thus, uncertainty about public debt had a direct impact on the investment decisions of private firms to the point of affecting the growth rate of the economy.

The reason why Italy's case was special, compared to other countries also experiencing episodes of uncertainty, is that Italy was sitting on a mountain of public debt, managed in conditions of incandescent political instability, turning into a potential earthquake with every shock.

At the beginning of the 1990s, major causes of economic uncertainty came from the corruption inquiries mentioned above, which more than ever before focused the attention of Italian policymakers and public on its domestic problems. Elected officials felt besieged by the judicial power, so much so that none of the political parties present in the Constitutional Assembly of 1946–1947 survived to the end of the decade. New parties were created, and new alliances were formed. The time-honored political discourse, based on right- and left-wing ideologies and on international alliances, was recast. Focused on themselves, Italians paid scanty attention to the global context and understood little of the revolutionary events reshaping the world's economy and geopolitics. It is enough to say that the liberalization of capital movement and the booming information and communication technologies required a new social contract aimed at redefining Italy's economic role in the world, the quality of its production, the development of its human capital, the predictability of administrative practices and the stability of the political response that presides over it all.

It would be unfair to affirm that the Italian political establishment was unaware of the size of the challenge underway. Between 1989 and 1992, the government anticipated the total liberalization of capital movement. This was done in full awareness that it was "a loss of sovereignty, exposing the political establishment to assessment by the international financial markets and Italian savers" (Carli 1996:395). Italy's public debt market was restructured, making it one of the most efficient in the world, but also one of the most interesting for foreign investors and their volatile trades. The lira's stability was defended on the exchange rate markets even when it was overvalued. The financial market was also structured and prepared to absorb the very large amount of assets derived from the process of privatization of state assets that would have changed the face of a fifty-year-old proto-capitalist system. The anti-trust regulation was finally adopted, and the central bank's autonomy was irrevocably established. The currency was linked more tightly to the exchange rate mechanism of the European monetary system, signaling to firms and trade unions that the wage and price inflation had to converge to the average European level. Automatic wage and pension indexations were removed, and with them, the informal social contract that had made Italians indifferent to sound monetary management. Fiscal balance was targeted to reduce the level of debt-to-GDP. It was a de facto reconnection – after almost thirty years – of Italy's political economy with the German postwar blueprint. All in all, the new social contract represented a revolution in the relationship between the citizens and the public powers, subjecting the latter's sovereignty to the conditions required to prosper in the global context. All this was made possible by Italy's harnessing its political economy to the nascent single European currency project through the enthusiastic adhesion to the Maastricht Treaty, thus endorsing the German model of "social market economy." Unfortunately, this ambitious transformative project failed in a matter of only twelve months, thrown overboard by the public persuasion that Italy's main and only problem was its corrupt political system and by a unique coincidence of multiple crises

The exceptional nature of the 1992 uncertainty, arising from the corruption scandals and high public debt, was that it was reinforced by four critical contextual events: (i) the exit, followed by a drastic devaluation, of the Italian lira and the British pound from the European Exchange Rate Mechanism, the monetary and currency framework within which Italy had tried for a decade to regain monetary stability and convergence with other European countries; (ii) the return after thirty years of the government accounts to a positive primary balance, which, simplifying, meant that the citizens were to pay higher taxes than the value of goods and services given to them by the state exactly in the moment when the credibility of the political system was at its lowest level; (iii) the bankruptcy of the EFIM, the third-largest state-owned industrial conglomerate, prompting the redesigning of the role of the state in the Italian economy; (iv) the barbaric killing in Palermo of two exemplary figures in the fight against the Mafia, public prosecutors Giovanni Falcone and Paolo Borsellino, an enormous blow to the citizens' confidence in the political establishment that was already crumbling under the "clean hands" inquiries.

The result of this unusual cluster of crises was the explosion of the citizens' latent, century-old lack of confidence in public authorities, which had profound consequences on the country's economy in the following decades.

4.4 The Citizens and the Crises

The first of the abovementioned crises occurred when it suddenly became impossible to keep the exchange rate of the lira within the boundaries established by the 1978 European Monetary System Agreement. In 1992, difficulties emerged in the economic unification of Eastern and Western Germany. The reduction in manufacturing production in the Eastern *Länder* made it clear that bringing the former German Democratic Republic up to speed would have taken much longer than anticipated after the fall of the Berlin Wall. On February 7, 1992, the Maastricht Treaty was signed. It was the founding act of the European Union, which specified not only the political and economic criteria for joining the Economic and Monetary Union (EMU), but set January 1, 1999 as the starting date of the single currency. The disagreements between the German government and the Bundesbank over the economic strategy, concerning both German reunification and the European Monetary Union, led the German central bank to take an extremist position: In July it brought the discount rate to 8.75 percent, the highest level since the war. For other European countries bound to keep the exchange rate fixed with the mark the increase in German rates came at a time when an ongoing slowdown in the international economy required a looser monetary policy. Italy was stuck between the desire to keep the value of the lira fixed and the lack of convergence of inflation in the previous years, resulting in the appreciation of the lira's real exchange rate.

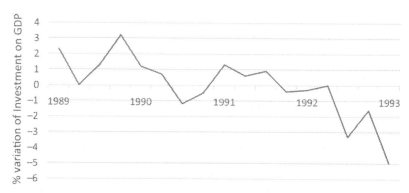

Figure 4.3 The 1992 shock on Italian investments (percentage of GDP)
Data source: OECD

The commitment of European countries to achieve the EMU had fueled the belief that laggard countries should implement the corrective measures necessary to converge with the German stability standards. From June 1992, however, the European integration process suffered a series of setbacks: the negative outcome of the Danish referendum to ratify the Maastricht Treaty, the tightening of German rates and the growing uncertainty about the outcome of the French referendum set for September 20. Against this backdrop, the markets expected that the exchange rates of the currencies of countries with high inflation would not hold. After more than five years of exchange rate stability, four 'realignments' (devaluations or revaluations) followed in just five months. On September 17, 1992, participation in the Exchange Rate Mechanism of the British pound and the Italian lira was suspended indefinitely. The pound would never return, in what appears now as a decisive precursor to Brexit. Episodes of acute turbulence followed one after the other until the first months of 1993 and then resumed in the following years.[5]

In the second half of 1992, the Italian economy entered a recession. The collapse of Italian investments, coinciding with the uncertainty surrounding the country's future, had an exceptional dimension (Fig. 4.3). It would have been difficult to observe a one-sixth drop in total investment in any advanced economy during just over a year. This was the first symptom of an era of investment instability that would continue in the following decades.

The fall in investments was concentrated in the medium and large industrial enterprises. In the spring of 1992, at the beginning of the political and judicial crisis that would upset the country, coinciding with the April elections, the sentiment of Italian entrepreneurs about their business perspectives took a sudden downward twist.

In 1992, investments in nonresidential construction, the most affected by judicial investigations, contracted sharply. The climate of suspicion toward all political parties paralyzed both private businesses and state-owned enterprises. The latter's investments declined by 18.6 percent compared to the 10.7 percent for private ones. Investment contraction was particularly pronounced in medium and large private companies. In firms with 200–999 employees, the investment shock was unprecedented, with a drop of nearly 25 percent. The profit margins of large companies fell to their lowest levels in twenty years. In 1993, investments saw a further decline of 8.8 percent, this time affecting small businesses more than proportionally. Investments suffered a heart attack across the board. A tide of pessimism about the future rolled from the top of the productive organizations down to the base of the business system. Bank of Italy Governor Antonio Fazio observed that the misallocation of resources caused by corruption "[was] proving to be of a frightening dimension" (Bank of Italy 1993).

In a context of public outrage toward politics and finance, the industrial and financial elite was paralyzed, as several of its leading exponents were subject to judicial inquiries and even arrested – perhaps a unique case in the history of capitalism. Silvio Berlusconi, a self-made media and real estate tycoon, reacted to the accusations by the Milanese prosecutors by, as he said, "descending into (the field of) politics" in October 1993. A few months later (May 1994), he won the elections and received the mandate to form the first of the three governments he would lead in the following two decades.

The climate of violent indignation in public opinion that followed the anti-corruption investigations was such that the media labeled the events as the end of the so-called First Republic and the beginning of the Second, as the dissolved historical political parties were replaced by new ones, in particular Berlusconi's "Forza Italia" (Go Italy) and the "Lega Nord" (Northern Italy), a secessionist party questioning the unity of the country and denouncing the "Southern mentality" of Italy's central governments. Leaders of the Lega Nord called on citizens to boycott government bond issuances. TV channels showed members of parliament queuing at the Chamber of Deputies' internal bank tellers to withdraw their savings. The relationship between politics, capitalism and public opinion took on a character of suspicion and antagonism that would remain, to say the least, latent in the country. Tensions that had been brewing in the earlier decades – based on regional differences, income inequality, the defense of privileges and much more – suddenly found voice in the indignation against the political class. The multitude of small entrepreneurs or self-employed workers identified with the populist overtones of Berlusconi's campaign, intolerant of the growing fiscal and bureaucratic burdens in a country that the corruption scandals had deprived of optimism and goodwill. In those years even the long decline in Italy's fertility rate had bottomed out (Fig. 4.4).

The importance of savings heightened the citizens' sensitivity toward financial instability. In 1992, among the seven major industrial countries, Italy had the highest public debt and the lowest household debt, equal to only 22 percent of GDP. The families' patrimonial position was therefore flourishing. The economic crisis, on the other hand, hit labor income, with a prospect of limited future wage increases following the agreements made in July 1992 by the government with the social partners. Furthermore, for the first time since the early 1970s and the third since the war, employment had decreased, by about 200,000 units.

In June 1992, after the constitution of the new government led by Giuliano Amato, a huge supplementary correction of the budget was implemented for an amount equal to almost 6 percent of GDP in an attempt to keep the borrowing requirements of the government under control and avoid the deterioration of expectations on the currency and financial markets. The fiscal intervention made it explicit to citizens and businesses what the depth and size were of the sacrifices needed to contain financial instability. Fears grew that exceptional and unpredictable measures could affect personal savings and wealth, from homes to bank deposits. Uncertainty about the nature of the assets that would be subject to taxation and fears about the involvement of government bonds increased doubts about the safety of households' financial wealth.

The climate of household confidence deteriorated rapidly, reaching its lowest point since 1982 in October, and consumption followed the trend. In 1993, Italy's gross domestic product declined by 0.7 percent, falling for the first time since 1975. Employment dropped (2.8 percent) with an intensity and speed that had been unprecedented in the

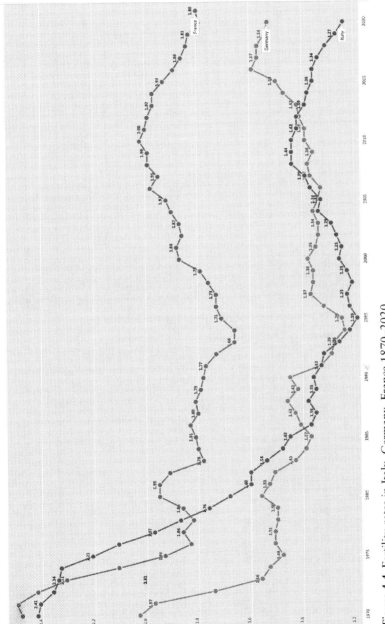

Figure 4.4 Fertility rates in Italy, Germany, France 1870–2020
Source of data: OECD

postwar period. Inequality in income distribution increased for the first time since the war.

The link between the debt crisis, financial instability and tax consequences on businesses and households became evident. Trying to stabilize the lira, the government for the first time in thirty years brought the primary budget balance (the borrowing requirement of the public administration, net of interest expenditure) back to surplus, raising fiscal pressure by more than 2 percent. Public expenditure other than that for interest and financial transactions continued to increase (+0.7 percent of GDP). In public opinion, the increase in the tax burden took on the character of a foregone result of all the various complications that the Italian economy had encountered.

In addition to the growing tax burden, the institutional crisis led to the hypertrophic production of rules and regulations as a reaction both to the inefficiency of the public administration and the capillary mechanisms of its corruption and collusion. The new regulatory burden was onerous for companies and tended to hinder rather than facilitate the approval of bureaucratic practices, to the point of unintentionally incentivizing companies and workers to hide in the shadow economy. A kind of vicious circle was established that increased the volume of both the rules and the subterfuges.

In 1992 a phase began in which the primary surplus of the Italian budget became permanently positive. In a few years, the balance went from 1.8 percent of the GDP in 1994 to 4.1 percent in 1996, and then up to 6.8 percent in 1997. The idea that for the foreseeable future Italians would have to give to the state more money than they would ever receive in return changed their attitude toward the state.

4.5 Southern Consequences of the Fiscal Policies

One of the least observed and most penetrating consequences of the new fiscal stance introduced after the 1992 crisis was its impact on the South. The South's economy proved hardly compatible with European financial stability and with a policy of public budget discipline. The 1980s had seen an increase in the South's economy's dependence on public transfers from the rest of Italy. A significant example came with the tragic earthquake in Irpinia, an area in the region of Campania bordering Calabria, on November 23, 1980. The reconstruction opened the way to an abuse of public funds so extensive as to multiply eightfold the taxpayer's costs, which exceeded €32 billion. The money, intermediated by local politicians, flowed into the wrong hands and was critical in strengthening emerging clans of organized crime.

In those years, there was also a shift from subsidies to production activities based in the South to direct subsidies to families. Through transfers and the payment of wages and salaries, the state budget generated 50 percent of household disposable income, and 60 percent of resource allocation. In 1992 the general policy of "extraordinary intervention" aimed at supporting economic activities in the South was scaled down, opening, until 1998, a phase in which the regional development policies in Italy became less intense.

The Southern Question ("*questione meridionale*"), managed for decades simply by transferring money, reemerged in the 1990s with the reduction of available resources from the state. In a way, the "question" epitomizes the historical flaws in the role of the state that we have described so far. According to Cassese (2019): "The North–South gap is not the result of insufficient investment or inadequate aid. Instead, it is the result of the shortage of social capital as well as the state's inability to produce collective goods: trust, rules governing coexistence, associative networks, aptitude for cooperation, civic culture." The anomie is produced by the scarce consistency of the social fabric, not counterbalanced by a well-ordered state capable of producing "equality under the law, procedures without exceptions, rules that cannot be twisted for the benefit of one and to the detriment of the other."

In more political terms, the new climate generated a "northernfica-tion" of the economy[6] and a "southernfication" of politics.[7] The conflict between the two orders of social intervention, in politics and in the economy, was just accompanying the widespread erosion of people's trust in politics that had been brewing for decades. As already mentioned, starting from the seventies, the deficit-to-GDP ratio of the South of Italy stayed well above 25 percent, with a peak of 35 percent, and then slowed down to 15 percent only in 1997.[8] To keep Italy's total deficit-to-GDP within the European fiscal limits (below 3 per-cent), starting from the end of the nineties the North was to maintain a surplus of 8–9 percent of its GDP and the Center of around 5 percent. It is no surprise that this asymmetry of contributions gave rise to strong regional resentments. Against the backdrop of its asymmetric burden, keeping the state's deficit below the Maastricht threshold eroded the original pro-European sentiment of the Italians.

In the North, the emergence of secessionist movements mirrored the cultural distance of the myriad of small entrepreneurs and millions of freelance workers from the central government in Rome and its tax exaction. Nobody embodied the spirit of the time better than Silvio Berlusconi, a media mogul from Milan who founded a successful party, Forza Italia, winning the elections in 1994. Berlusconi's populist vocation and personal vitalism marked a break with the process of Europeanization that Italy had begun at the end of the 1980s. He shunned the idea of aligning the country's modernization with European rules and fiscal discipline. Driven by personal business interests, Berlusconi fought law enforcement with tailor-made laws and strong rhetoric against judicial powers and state taxation, at the same time underestimating the new challenges arising from globalization.

5 | *The Lost Opportunity, 1996–2007*

5.1 The Second Divergence

The crisis of 1992–1993 was not dramatic if measured in terms of economic growth. The GDP's decline by more than 1 percent was followed by two years of relatively robust growth (2.5 percent per year). The year 1995 saw maximum convergence of the Italian per capita income and labor productivity with the leading developed countries. Measured in terms of purchasing power parity, that is, taking into account the different costs of goods and services in individual countries, Italy's per capita GDP was then equal to 71 percent of the United States level, about 90 percent of the German, and roughly the same as that of Great Britain and France (Table 1.3).

Italy's economic history changed radically in the following twelve years. After a century of convergence, the country embarked on a second long phase of economic divergence from the main European countries and the United States. Between 1995 and 2007, Italy's GDP grew on average by 1.4 percent yearly, considerably less than in the other countries we have referred to so far, so that by 2007, the last year before the Great Recession, Italy's income per inhabitant had fallen to 62 percent of that of the US, 85 percent of the British and 88 percent of the French. The gap with Germany, grappling with a colossal restructuring operation after the shock of the reunification, narrowed only a bit. Except for a short time, between 2005 and 2007, the Italian manufacturing industry experienced a period of virtual stagnation (growth was only 0.3 percent per year).

Between 1995 and 2007, product (GDP) per hour worked, measured at purchasing power parity, fell from 100 to 85 percent of that of the United States (Fig. 3.1) and lost ground to the major European countries. Even at a time when all advanced countries experienced productivity slowdowns, the virtual stagnation of Italian product per hour worked stands out as the most telling indicator of the difficulties of its economy.

Some structural factors help explain the reasons why an economy that had successfully caught up with the more economically developed countries became an economy that moved away from them, growing at much slower rates.

Against the new international backdrop, the often inefficient and opaque management both of small and medium-sized family-run enterprises, the low degree of competition in the internal market for services and strong geographical dualism had a more negative impact on growth than in the previous decades.

The share of adults aged twenty-five to sixty-four holding a tertiary education degree was 36 percent in the United States, around 30 percent in Japan, the United Kingdom, Sweden, Finland and Belgium, while in Italy it was only 10 percent, with a large portion of the population having dropped out of school all together. The proportion of new graduates in engineering and other scientific disciplines was the lowest among the major industrial countries. The low average level of education of the Italian population did not matter much in the prevailing Fordist technology environment, requiring only a handful of good engineers and a normally educated working force. It became crucially relevant in the diffusion and adaptation of information and communication technology, for which the existence of a large number of tertiary-educated people is essential (Fig. 5.1).

The size, scope and productivity of the large firms had diminished in the 1980s. In the last two decades of the twentieth century, Italy's large firms had relied on financial development rather than investing in products and innovations. Since large companies are the best positioned to compete internationally in the high-tech sectors and the most capable of investing in research, with positive fallouts and externalities on the small and medium-sized enterprises, their reduced number and size were bound to hurt productivity growth.

The traditionally rigid and segmented labor market, coupled with a welfare state focused on old-age pensions, inefficient in favoring labor mobility through adequate unemployment benefits and retraining, was also a liability at a time when technology and labor organization required flexible labor markets. Job precariety was bound to become socially disruptive in the absence of adequate welfare provisions to reduce uncertainty for individuals, families and local communities.

Finally, at the beginning of the 1990s, an exceptionally high public debt-to-GDP ratio required drastic fiscal policy changes with economic

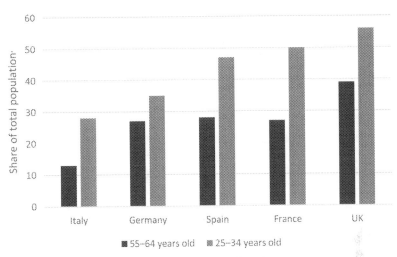

Figure 5.1 Share of population with tertiary education
Data source. OECD (2020) *Education at a glance*, Paris

as well as social impacts. The disruptive confidence crisis in the political class darkened investors' sentiments and moved many of them away from new businesses, shifting their focus on real estate businesses or other low-risk activities.

5.2 The Vicious Circle: Debt and Uncertainty

With the 1992 devaluation, the last of the lira, the currency lost about one-third of its value. Given the nostalgia that some Italians have for the times before the euro, it is appropriate to consider the effects of those devaluations. The impact on the real economy was an energetic, but not lasting, support for exporting manufacturing companies. The financial impact, instead, was different from the past: In the new context of capital mobility, businesses and households rushed to diversify their portfolios, bringing the country close to a dangerous spiral between capital flight and debt default.

With the instability of the lira, companies had been increasingly investing part of their revenues abroad. "Portfolio diversification" had become a common attitude among savings-rich Italian families as well.

During and after the shocks of 1992, the internationalization of enterprises became so frenetic that it resembled a flight from the country. The number of foreign affiliates of Italian groups increased from 180 in 1991 to 700 in 2001. The phenomenon involved the same medium and large companies that had stopped investing at home in 1992. Traditional sectors, such as textiles, clothing, specialized mechanical engineering, housewares, food and steel, organized themselves into pocket multinationals in search of the new markets that were opening throughout the world.[1] The flight away from Italy was underlined by the dramatic alarm launched by the Bank of Italy: "Toward the end of 1994 (Italy) came close to a perverse spiral of capital flight, devaluation of the exchange rate, acceleration of prices, fall in the prices of securities" (Bank of Italy 1995).

As mentioned, the impact of the devaluation on the real economy was strong. Between 1992 and 1995, exports increased in volume by 35 percent, although the result in value was much lower precisely because the prices in lira corresponded to fewer marks or dollars. The devaluation rewarded first the mature "Made in Italy" sectors – tiles, clothing, washing machines and others – in which the selling price of the product was an important factor of competitiveness. In the early 1990s, when fundamental technological innovations were being produced and spread throughout the world, the devaluation of the lira disadvantaged the high-tech sectors, where non-price factors matter most and in which the Italian balance of payments showed a deficit. It was not until 1995 that Italian companies invested for the first time in information technologies long established in the United States. On average, in the 1990s, Italian companies in the critical sectors of chemicals, pharmaceuticals and avionics had fallen behind by seven years in adopting technology already in use in the United States (Bugamelli and Pagano 2004). In information and communication technology, the country had "missed the train" after the collapse of Olivetti and the unstable success of publicly controlled companies that had identified the right sectors already in the 1960s. With the new international agreements under the aegis of the World Trade Organization (WTO), it had become more difficult to "import" innovations from other countries, often simply by copying them, and to climb the technological ladder without being equipped with large structures with their own research and development and, as it was common for Italian firms, devoting on average the equivalent of only 1 percent of GDP to those expenses.

According to research by the School of European Political Economy at LUISS University based on data published by Istat (2016: 10),

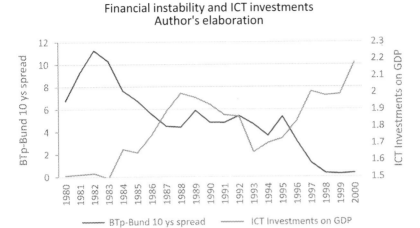

Figure 5.2 Financial instability and ICT investments in Italy
Data from: FRED Economic Data (Federal Reserve Bank of St. Louis); and EU Klem

investments in research and intellectual property or software have been negatively correlated with the degree of political and economic uncertainty in the country. This correlation may be the most important factor in Italy's recent economic history. In the wake of the shocks of 1992, Italy's public debt became an intractable amplifier of political and financial instability, and its cost – measured in terms of interest rate differential versus the German bonds – turned out to be the most significant inhibitor of technological investments (Fig. 5.2).

Large holdings of Italy's risky government bonds made bank port-folios riskier, reducing credit availability for loans, particularly those granted to fund research and technology investments. The reason why banks were not willing to make such loans was their "non-physical" (intangible) nature, that is, that they were not guaranteed by collateral that the bank could recover in case the research failed to produce revenue. Moreover, funding for those investments normally yields in the longer term, making them riskier in the short term. Once political instability was mirrored in the instability of the public debt, a vicious circle set in whereby poor technology hindered productivity, and low productivity lowered economic growth making the debt-to-GDP ratio rise further. Higher taxes were needed to finance the public debt, with the consequence, once more, of hindering growth and increasing political instability.

All this happened in the decade when the global economic system moved away from material products toward new intangible products in artificial intelligence and other advanced applications. Political uncertainty, the fall in investments and the dramatic devaluation played against Italy's reconnection with the more advanced economies. Since then, Italian productivity has lost pace with the rest of the world. Between 1995 and 2000, the annual increase in hourly labor productivity in the US industry was 4.5 percent. In France, it was even higher (4.6 percent), almost double compared to Germany (2.4 percent). But in Italy in the same years, the average annual increase in product per hour in the manufacturing sector stopped at 0.9 percent.

Institutional stability proved to be a critical factor for the Italian economy. While the shocks of 1992 represented a permanent spoke in the wheel for Italian society, an attempt to recover ground in investments, specifically in the technological ones crucial for productivity, coincided with the prospect of the country finally entering a stable European monetary framework. Around 1998, when Italy gained access to the euro, investments in ICT (Information and Communications Technology) finally made a positive contribution to the growth of the economy. However, after a couple of years, uncertainty set in again, and ICT's contribution to Italian development declined once more.

Italy's delay in adopting new technologies was partly due to the reduced weight of large private companies. Legislative innovations supported the momentum of medium-sized enterprises that had begun in the 1980s, aiming at consolidating enterprises in a more competitive context. The first antitrust legislation was introduced in 1990, over forty years after the establishment of the Bundeskartellamt in Germany. In 1991 parliament passed legislation safeguarding the development of the "industrial districts," agglomerations of single productions organized in a horizontal and vertical division of labor typical of the Italian social and productive fabric. There were 190 districts, mainly distributed between Northern and Central Italy, where a professional legacy, in some cases dating back to the medieval guilds, was still alive or encouraged by a modern entrepreneurial attitude and work ethic.

Some of the "Made in Italy" companies managed in the following years to make the leap from pure exporters to multinationals. They were almost always family businesses, albeit often with management hired from outside, but their size remained below those of their global competitors. For many of them, the reluctance to grow, invest or introduce more advanced technologies proved to be a factor of disadvantage if compared to their European and global competitors. Family control also made merger operations difficult. The absence of adequate financial intermediaries to accompany the internationalization of companies made it even more difficult to fully exploit the size of the newly globalized markets.[2]

To defuse the negative effects of the devaluations, the government adopted income policies that slowed the upsurge of wage inflation. The dramatic depreciation of the lira and the loss, between July 1992 and January 1994, of over one million jobs (both phenomena of an intensity never experienced in the postwar period) could have triggered stagflation. As a result of the devaluation, the prices in lira of imported materials had increased by almost 20 percent. However, Italy's society demonstrated its reactivity: A fundamental agreement was signed by the representatives of firms, trade unions and the government in July 1993 to advance the process of labor contracts reform that had already begun with the agreement of July 1992. A new era opened in the relations between capital and labor, abandoning the conflictual attitudes of the past. After 1992, the definitive cessation of the "*scala mobile*" (automatic wage indexation) mechanism was accepted by the trade unions, establishing the principle that wage bargaining should be divided into "non-overlapping and distinct" levels, sectoral or corporate. With the 1993 agreement, firms and trade unions undertook to make contracts consistent with the macroeconomic objectives set by the government. Wage negotiation could thus be aimed at combating inflation *ex ante*, rather than running after it, with the risk of fueling it.

Finally, devaluations had nonuniform effects on the national economic geography. About 85 percent of the exporting manufacturing capacity was located in the Northern and Central regions. The marginalization in the economic geography of the Southern regions coincided with the shock caused by the Mafia's brutal killing of judges Falcone and Borsellino, creating a sense of estrangement in the North. While other less advanced economies were rapidly and successfully catching up, the hope of re-engaging the South with the ongoing global economic process took a hard blow.

Over the following decades, countries like Poland, which in 1995 had a per capita income less than half of Italy's, managed to exceed both the income and education levels of Italy's poorest

Southern regions, as well as their level of productivity and trade integration with the rest of Europe. The quality differences between the Fiat plants in Poland and those in the South (Pomigliano and Termini Imerese), or even the old plant in Turin (Mirafiori), became evident in the 1990s. Italy as a low-cost provider of industrial components, at least relative to other Western European competitors, found tough competition in Eastern European countries receiving massive subsidies from the European institutions and directly from Italy itself. The fiscal and social security contribution burden on labor was felt in the context of growing tax competition. The Italian tax-on-GDP rate was at a level between that of Germany and France (respectively, 43 and 48 percent of GDP), significantly higher than that of the United States (32 percent) and the United Kingdom (37 percent).

While in Italy, between 1980 and 1997, the tax rate on the profits of joint-stock companies rose from 36 to 53 percent, other large countries were reducing the rates on business activities. Italian corporate tax rates reached Germany's high levels, surpassing those of France and the United Kingdom.

5.3 Privatizations and the Restructuring of Italian Capitalism

The liberalization of the banking system and the privatization of government-controlled companies, starting with IRI and ENI, played an important role in the radical discontinuity in Italian economic development that started in 1992.[3]

The spur for changing the banking system came once again from the European Community, which in the 1980s had forcefully fought against state aid, distorting competition in the Single Market. Until 1992, the Italian banking system was almost entirely in the hands of the state, or under its influence, as in the case of the three major credit institutions, the "banks of national interest" – Banca Commerciale Italiana, Banco di Roma and Credito Italiano – owned by IRI. Moreover, the post-1992 recession led to the systemic crisis of the Southern banks, with the de facto bankruptcy of the Banco di Napoli and the reform of the savings banks.

New dynamism in the "petrified forest"[4] of Italian banks, still governed by the banking law of 1936, was imparted by the so-called Amato Law of 1990.[5] Overall, the set of regulatory and tax incentives resulted in a formidable boost to bank mergers. In the 1990s, about

500 aggregation operations were carried out. The five largest groups came to control 50 percent of the market. The Italian banking system was strengthened, but it was strengthened by increasing the power of a few banks that assumed the improper role of "systemic banks," aiming at a relevant role in the defense of Italy's economic interests. A similar role was gradually imitated by smaller regional banks, "systemic" in their territorial context. As we will see, the efficiency in the allocation of credit to the Italian economy increased on average, though preserving some old habits in their credit allocation practices.

The privatization program tickled large companies' opportunism and made them engage again in the domestic economy. Large firms were also encouraged by the prospect of Italy's participation in the European Economic and Monetary Union, which promised to bring about a stabler monetary and fiscal framework.

The relationship between the state and large companies has a long and complex tradition in Italy, but what happened in the 1990s, with the state's desperate need to sell its corporate stakes, was not a noble chapter in the book of Italian capitalism. Let us take as an example the description of the Telecom case offered by economist Marco Onado. The telephone company had to play a fundamental role, at a time when information and communication technologies were expanding throughout the rest of the world. "The mother of all privatizations ... did not have a safety net constituted by shareholders willing to invest in the long term. The Fiat group, which through IFIL had acquired 0.6 percent of the capital, not only claimed to run the company but immediately showed that it was interested in power for the sake of power, rather than industrial strategies" (Onado 2014).

Later, Roberto Colaninno, a manager from the sector, took over from IFIL the control of the telecom company and loaded it with an enormous debt, 60 trillion lire (about €30bn), necessary to finance his takeover bid. Onado (2014) writes again:

The control of the new Telecom is exercised with the traditional weapons of Italian relationship capitalism: a beautiful chain of pyramid companies .... At the end of July 2001, one of Italy's leading industrialists, Marco Tronchetti Provera, bought the Telecom shares through a corporate pyramid, without the need to launch a takeover bid. In the end, Telecom's debts were twice as large as its assets and weighed on the group's wings. A further equity sale was necessary. Telecom ended up in the hands of a composite group that included the largest Italian banks alongside Spanish Telefónica.

The net effect was a dramatic decline in the profitability of what had been the telecommunications giant at the forefront of global mobile communication, losing billions over the subsequent years.

Large companies were losing dynamism in the world economy, in which internationalization and research acquired greater importance. Attracted by other opportunities in the opening global economy, foreign investors lost interest in Italy's market. The balance of direct investments was strongly negative in the five-year period (1992–1996). The opening of the Eastern European markets made the German chains of subcontractors move from Italy to the Czech Republic, Slovakia, Poland, Hungary and Romania, countries with similar industrial vocations, but with much lower labor costs. Many Italian producers also shifted their new investments abroad, making Italy the second-largest foreign investor in Eastern Europe after Germany. While wage-contracts renewals in Germany took note of the new competition from beyond the Eastern borders, in Italy wage costs continued to rise despite the stagnation of productivity.

The restructuring process of Italian capitalism should be evaluated in parallel with that of German capitalism, a system with the same tax burden, though with a different public infrastructure setup. Germany and Italy had, and still have, the two largest manufacturing sectors in Europe but their choices in the 1990s could not have been more different. In the mid-1990s, Germany was at the height of the difficulties resulting from unification between the former West and East. The balance of payments, historically in significant surplus, turned negative in 1996. In the meantime, however, the major industrial groups underwent profound internal restructuring, taking advantage of the possibilities offered by the relocation of production to the countries of Eastern Europe and then Asia. Under global competition and the adoption of "shareholder value" managerial practices, relations between capital and labor radically changed. Trade unions chose to defend employment levels rather than wage rigidity. In the same years, partly traumatized by political and financial instability, a large part of Italian capitalism preferred to invest in traditional activities, exploiting privatizations also to invest in public utility companies hitherto run by public monopolists: Fiat and Pirelli invested in telecommunications and real estate; De Benedetti in banking and telecommunications; Benetton in highways and food chains; Riva in the steel industry and so on, looking mostly within national borders for sectors that were still partly protected from competition or regulated by the counterpart in privatization. The aggressive restructuring of German capitalism coincided with the vigorous development of globalization and, to a lesser extent, with the spread of new information technologies originating in the United States, a sector in which Italian capitalism arrived belatedly and reluctantly.

In November 1996, the lira rejoined the European Exchange Rate Mechanism (ERM). By then, despite all the abovementioned difficulties, competitiveness, based on production prices, exceeded the level of 1992 by 8 percent. The recovery of demand had managed to revitalize corporate fixed investments, which rebounded in 1994 and 1995. However, the benefits of the devaluation were already running out. In the second half of 1996 it became evident that annual GDP growth would not exceed 1 percent and industrial production was in decline.

With the last devaluation Italy also entered a new political dimension. In the previous decades, distributional conflicts between labor and capital were normally mirrored by an excessive increase in consumption or, alternatively, an excessive accumulation of savings. If distributional conflicts end in excessive consumption, the result can be the growth of imports and the inflow of capital bringing a deficit in the balance of payments, which can be temporarily remedied through the devaluation of the currency. In a way, distributional conflicts could only continue in the framework of flexible exchange rates.

The end of the devaluations would have required the Left and the Right, or labor and capital, to change their conflictual rhetoric because a deficit (or an excessive surplus) of the balance of payments, resulting from the distributional conflict, was no more curable letting the exchange rate fluctuate. Thus, labor and capital should have worked in a common effort to sustain economic growth. In this regard, a change of mentality partly occurred but it was not designed to improve the technological quality of Italy's productions. Significantly, an indicator of the efficient combination of labor and capital – total factor productivity – showed that Italy was losing ground.

Rather than discussing together the necessary reforms, political poles preferred to resort to other forms of harsh antagonism, centered now on the judicial predicaments of the governing elite.

5.4 Excluded from the Euro?

If the multiple crises of 1992 were a powerful factor of instability for the country's economy and society, the answer in terms of stabilization was offered by the prospect of solid financial anchoring to the European framework through the confirmation of the monetary union process. The urge to reach the convergence criteria defined in the Maastricht Treaty (public deficit below 3 percent of GDP and public debt gradually approaching 60 percent) in order to participate in the single currency from the outset became the main reference point for Italy's political economy and a popular issue for Italian public opinion.

The political and symbolic objective – the Italians commonly spoke not of "entering the euro" but of "entering Europe" – of joining the single currency prevailed over the necessary reflection on the reforms of the society and the economy that would have allowed Italy to reap the benefits of the stable monetary framework granted by the euro. On the contrary, as soon as Italy's accession to the single currency was guaranteed, the effort to make the country's institutional structure more efficient – through a bicameral commission in which both government and opposition parties would participate – was abandoned.

In 1997, the Prodi government achieved a sizable budget result. The primary surplus, which had already increased from 1.8 percent of the domestic product in 1994 to 4.1 percent in 1996, rose to 6.8 percent in 1997. During those three years, the public sector's deficit declined from 9.2 to 6.7 and 2.7 percent of GDP, below the fateful threshold of 3 percent required by the European Union. However, the progress made in extremis in 1997 was due to the increase of the tax burden (by approximately 2 percentage points) and to other measures having in part the nature of postponing expenses.

Despite the remarkable decline of the state budget deficit, Italy entered the single currency with a very heavy public budgetary situation both in terms of expenditure and revenue. In the European Union, average total public expenditure in relation to the Gross Domestic Product was around 48 percent in the 1980s and reached a peak of 53 percent in 1993. In Italy, starting from 42 percent of GDP in 1980, spending was close to 58 percent in 1993. The Italian tax burden, which in 1980 was at a much lower level than in other countries, came to exceed the European average (43 percent), reaching 44 percent in 1997. Italian fiscal efforts had been extraordinary and generally accepted by citizens, including the adoption of the famous "Eurotax," a temporary tax intended precisely to bring the public deficit below 3 percent of GDP by 1997. Yet, despite their very rapid growth, tax revenues always lagged spending, as had been the case since 1913. Overall, Italy entered the single currency with total public spending in 1997 equal to about 51.5 percent of GDP and with a public debt of around 114 percent. Under these conditions, the lira's transformation into the euro became possible only thanks to the determination of the Prodi government and its Minister of Economy, Carlo Azeglio Ciampi, who considered the operation vital for the stabilization of the country's political and economic conditions.

Only a minority of governments and a small portion of public opinion in the rest of Europe favored Italy's participation in the monetary union. German Chancellor Helmut Kohl held out for a long time before giving a cautious green light against the energetic opposition of Bundesbank Governor Hans Tietmeyer and the vast majority of German public opinion.

One episode demonstrates how difficult it was for Italy to join the euro. The last step involved approval by the governors of the national central banks meeting in the governing council of the European Monetary Institute (EMI), the institution from which the European Central Bank would be constituted. The choice of the admitted countries was to be made on March 24, 1998, and communicated in the morning after through the publication of an EMI report, assessing the compliance of the candidate countries with the entry criteria. The original version of the EMI report gave a negative assessment of Italy's qualification for admission, arguing that Italy's high public debt was a cause of "serious concern." The governors, including Italian Central Bank Governor Antonio Fazio, were against Italy's admission and formally sanctioned its exclusion from the first round of countries admitted to the euro. If disregarded, their assessment would have been used by the German Constitutional Court to prevent Germany from taking part in the euro. The report was to remain secret until the morning after the meeting, but the seal was surprisingly broken by an Italian newspaper article before midnight, a few hours before the report had to be printed and made public. In the following frenetic hours, Finance Minister Ciampi grabbed the phone and convinced the EMI governors – former colleagues of his when he was at the helm of the Bank of Italy – to revoke their decision and correct the text with the more harmless "ongoing concern" phrase, the same judgment assigned to Belgium (then with a higher debt-to-GDP ratio than Italy). The change in the report's wording eventually paved the way to Italy's participation in the single currency.[6]

Having remained on the tightrope until the last minute, Italy eventually went on to become one of the eleven EU states that adopted the single currency. From January 1, 1999, the central banks of the eleven countries and the European Central Bank consolidated their balance sheets for monetary policy purposes. The interest rate on the transactions was the same for all countries, and the liabilities of each central bank, redenominated in euros, became interchangeable without any limit.

The concern for the evolution of Italian public accounts was justified. The 1998 Economic and Financial Planning Document of the Italian government had already outlined a less rigorous trajectory of debt reduction. The reduction in the deficit-to-GDP ratio was projected to slow down from 2.6 percent of GDP forecast in 1998 to 2.0 percent in 1999, 1.5 percent in 2000 and 1.0 percent in 2001. Italy's primary surplus declined from 6.8 percent in 1997 to 5.5 percent in 1998, still a remarkable level. A rapid reduction of the Italian public debt would have required maintaining such a minimum target for at least a decade. Unfortunately, this did not happen.

5.5 The Half-Caught Benefits of the Euro

The attempt to rebalance Italy's economic policy in the 1990s was considerable in its dimensions. Some macroeconomic stability had been achieved for the first time in decades, and the deficit of the public sector declined from 11.1 percent of the GDP in 1990 to 1.9 percent at the end of the decade. Inflation dropped from close to 10 percent in the 1980s to an average of 3.9 percent in the 1990s, reaching 1.7 percent in 1999. Long-term interest rates fell from levels well above 10 percent in the early 1990s to below 5 percent in 1999. However, it was clear that the country's position was far from secure and that its economic structure would still require reforming. In the second half of the 1990s, world trade grew in volume by 28 percent, but the increase in Italian exports was only 10 percent despite the great 1992–1995 devaluation. The GDP increased by only 6 percent over the same period, and imports by 24 percent. In the other ten euro countries, GDP grew by 9.5 percent, while exports and imports had both increased by 31 percent. The growth in industrial production between 1995 and 1999 was only about a third of the other countries.

The low export growth highlighted the competitiveness problem. On the one hand, the increase in unit costs was linked to the devaluations;

on the other hand, wage increases did not correspond to productivity increases. Measured on producer prices, the loss of competitiveness between 1993 and 1999 was 2.3 percentage points. In the same period, the competitiveness of industry in Germany had instead marked an improvement of 7 percentage points and in France of 8.

There are several reasons for this loss of competitiveness: a lack of innovation that should probably be traced back to the financial and institutional shocks of 1992, a time when new information technologies were being developed. Furthermore, in the second half of the decade, labor remunerations exceeded productivity growth by 12 percentage points (in France the increase in labor costs was 4.4 points lower than that of productivity, while in Germany it was 5 points lower).

Finally, high taxes and low productivity widened the gap between rising unit labor costs and the real wages of employees. Household disposable income dropped by about 5 percent and inequality in the distribution of income increased. Families defended their levels of consumption by reducing their savings. Companies, on the contrary, considered the shocks of 1992, the subsequent fiscal policies and the absence of further devaluations as reasons for concern about the future, which all led them to limit product supply or take refuge in traditional, less innovative sectors.

The problem was not so much the amount of investment, but rather their quality. Indeed, the loss of competitiveness was partly due to the type and quality of Italian products, unfit to respond to the growing demand for high-tech goods. The demand for those goods was growing worldwide at twice the rate of that for other products; the share of total exports of manufactured goods in the decade had remained unchanged in Italy at 8 percent, while it had risen from 13 to 19 percent in the European Union and 26 to 29 percent in the United States.

We must return here to the global scenario that appeared in the late 1980s with the end of the "great divergence" and the return of the Asian continent to the market economy. To deal with competition from China or India, economic systems in which labor costs were very low and the level of social protection minimal, western companies had to move toward products and services with higher added value, those which were technologically advanced or had high qualitative levels. The Italian state should have encouraged citizens' education and professional training

(Visco 2014). Furthermore, to shift resources from less productive to more productive firms, a less rigid regulation of labor relations, a closer link between wages and productivity and a more effective welfare system would have been necessary. On the contrary, Italy continued to stand out for its very low ratio between official workers and the total labor force. In the euro area the employment rate was 60 percent, in Italy it was 52, and in the South only 41 percent. The inefficiency of Italy's labor market was striking in the number of irregular workers with significantly lower than average remuneration and no social coverage. Their number increased significantly after Italy joined the euro. Despite everything, we will see that within a few years Italy would have an opportunity to resume a faster growth trajectory.

After joining the euro, the Italian economy had to take up the challenge of global competition by engaging in an unprecedented process of "creative destruction," that is, facilitating the replacement of obsolete activities with those more able to grow in the new context. However, during Berlusconi's 2001–2005 period as prime minister, the country plunged into a climate of internal controversy that stifled the understanding of the new global challenges the country was facing. Thus, despite the longer duration of the legislatures and governments, the degree of uncertainty about the country's future did not diminish. From the mid-1990s on, after each election, the country saw an alternation of political majorities with conflicting orientations in economic policy and their relationship with Europe.

A brilliant entrepreneur, Berlusconi was also the most visible relic of old political patronage, condemned for corruption and tax evasion, and even suspected of connections with the Sicilian Mafia. Since the early 1990s he had become the target of obsessive judicial activity that grew more rabid once it was clear the TV mogul was the only hurdle barring the way to power for the Left parties flanking the judges. The fight between Berlusconi and the judicial powers absorbed the rhetoric of the country in full. Heavier taxation and burdensome regulation conjured a sentiment in favor of the insouciant billionaire, legendarily hedonistic, who promised everyone a happy life that was in complete contrast with the rigor and sacrifice called by his political opponents.

In the first decade of the new century, Italy changed its destiny by missing the opportunity offered by a favorable international economic context to reduce its public debt before the onset of the 2008 global crisis. In those years, the quality of political choices was not up to the global challenges. Between 2000 and 2009, each year actual GDP growth was lower than had been expected, despite benign external circumstances (Bastasin et al. 2019). The average growth of "total factor productivity," a synthetic indicator of the efficiency with which capital and labor combine in the production process, was negative (−0.9 percent). This figure summarizes Italy's poor ability to introduce new technologies and its lack of dynamism in moving capital and labor toward the best allocation of resources. Those years revealed Italy's poor political will and capacity to carry out the necessary reforms.

After the launch of the euro, a part of the industrial system adjusted to the new competitive environment by adopting a global scale or improving its production processes.[7] Another part of the industrial system was instead overwhelmed by the new competitive context. The banking system preferred to grant indiscriminate loans to real estate developers, many of whom were destined for bad business and a bad personal fate, rather than to the innovative firms. About 40 percent of bank loans in the first years of the euro ended up in the real estate sector, residential or commercial, and related activities. Families were inclined to invest their savings in real estate to protect themselves from what they felt was an inflationary push coinciding with the introduction of the euro. Although the statistics do not confirm the increase in the price index, anecdotal evidence shows cases in which the euro exchange rate was translated into one euro per thousand lire, instead of being converted to 1,936.27 lire. The citizen's sense of distrust was aggravated.

While in Italy businesses and families were dealing with bricks and mortar, the establishment of "global value chains" was underway on a planetary scale that redesigned the world's productive networks. Investments in ICT allowed companies to allocate parts of their production processes in different locations on a global scale.[8]

After 2003, the country's introversion became evident: Parliament was paralyzed by an ongoing acrimonious fight around the figure of Prime Minister Silvio Berlusconi and his problems with justice. The financial system, used to collusive practices, could not withstand the opening of borders. The arrival of foreign investors in the Italian banking market provoked a protectionist reaction by the Bank of Italy so controversial that it led to investigations by the judiciary and the traumatic resignation of Governor Antonio Fazio with his replacement by Mario Draghi.

5.6 The Success of Creative Destruction

The country seemed politically immobile. The reforms, necessary for the evolution of Italian capitalism, were not carried out in the first decade of the century. This is a crucial point. The ability to be more or less competitive does not seem to be linked only to innovative sectors as opposed to mature ones, because even in the latter there were cases of strong increases in productivity due to the adoption of new technologies. In each sector, very productive companies coexisted alongside very inefficient ones (Schivardi 2018). Resources, workers, skills and capital should have shifted from inefficient firms to better ones, capable of guaranteeing higher wages. These transfers – hampered by labor rigidity and the lack of capital dynamics – did not occur in Italy (Calligaris et al. 2018).

The changes in the structure of capitalism and the different priorities in a context of greater competition led the business front to split in the first decade of the twenty-first century when the presidency of Confindustria, the powerful industrialists' association, for the first time was not controlled by large companies, whose main shareholders were distancing themselves from the country. Within a few years, Fiat moved its center of gravity to America and its corporate and tax offices to Amsterdam and London. Pirelli was sold to a Chinese group. Luxottica split between Italy and France. Even then Prime Minister Berlusconi's holding Mediaset moved to Holland. The leadership of the Industrial Confederation was conquered by small or medium-sized entrepreneurs who sided politically with Berlusconi and his program of disregard for European rules, decriminalization of false accounting, liberalization of the labor market and reduction of corporate taxes.

The choice was important because it opened a phase, not the first one in the history of Italy, which can be defined as "partisan protectionism" (Bastasin 2015): In the face of globalization, Right and Left politics were returning to traditional categories of capital (Right) and labor (Left), liberalizing only the adverse factor of production (the Right liberalized labor and the Left did the same with businesses) and protecting their own.[9] It was in those years that, not surprisingly, the unusual and sharp fall in the "total factor productivity" took place.

Despite all the difficulties, the bulk of the Italian economy remained vital and carried out a turnaround in the activity of businesses that few would have foreseen, one that became visible around the middle of the decade. A survey conducted in 2006 by the Bank of Italy on a sample of over 4,000 companies reported that "over half of the industrial companies had changed their strategy in the first five years of the century. The 12 percent that had shifted the product range to new sectors had higher than average profits. One in five companies, an almost double share compared to the beginning of the decade, adopted forms of internationalization" (Brandolini and Bugamelli 2009). In all companies, the importance of investments in planning, design, brands, distribution and assistance networks had increased. New technologies for integrated business management were spreading among the medium-large firms and the use of personnel with higher levels of education also increased. These were concrete signs of the Italian industrial system's turn in the direction required by the global challenge.

The euro triggered a virtuous mechanism for the reorganization of productive activity. Contrary to the hypothesis that the discipline imposed by the euro triggered the competitiveness crisis of Italian companies, the evidence indicates that acting within a "stable" currency regime was an incentive for companies to increase efficiency. According to estimates by the Bank of Italy, productivity gains, which may reflect both the reallocation of resources within sectors and improved efficiency by individual companies, were not accompanied by a reduction in employment. The liberalization of the labor market, with the introduction of new "flexible" contractual figures, made it possible to combine corporate reorganization with a significant decrease in the unemployment rate.

The real missed opportunity, however, was not so much that of industrial modernization, which remained confined to a minority of companies successful in international markets, but, as we will see, the missed opportunity for stabilization of Italy's public finance.

5.7 The Destructive Part of the Process

It would be wrong to say that in 2007 the productivity and competitiveness problems of the 1990s had been overcome. Productivity in industry, which fell by 3 percentage points between 2001 and 2005, grew by just over one point in 2006, while in Germany, France and Spain it rose between 3 and 6 percent. The gap in unit labor cost dynamics continued to grow. And, unlike a part of the system that reacted positively but could not expand sufficiently, another part seemed to give up on productivity growth (Micossi 2017).

At the end of 2003, food giant Parmalat went bankrupt, involving hundreds of companies all over the world. Airway carrier Alitalia required state money to remain active: In 2004 the Treasury granted a guarantee on a bridge loan of 400 million euros and in 2006 the privatization process was started, followed by a new bailout in 2008 implemented to prevent the sale of the company to a foreign bidder, Air France, opposed by Silvio Berlusconi's "chauvinistic" election campaign. Even Fiat, the country's largest industrial group, found itself on the verge of bankruptcy in the mid-2000s, unable to evolve from an Italian-centered business model, with low-quality products and close relations to the public administration and under the umbrella protection of a friendly financial network run by investment bank Mediobanca. It was Sergio Marchionne, a complete outsider whose family had migrated to Canada and had never worked in Italy, who saved Fiat and turned it into a modern multinational company.

Another symptom of institutional fragility was the increase in the underground economy. According to estimates based on the use of cash, between 2005 and 2008 the black or illegal economy increased by an astounding 6.6 percent of GDP.[10]

Organized crime also crept into this reality, assuming unprecedented dimensions not only in the South. From money laundering, the Mafia and other criminal organizations – the Camorra and 'Ndrangheta – expanded into the management of public procurement, through the infiltration of their affiliates, and then into the acquisition of private companies, particularly in catering and construction.

A destructive phase also involved the banking sector. Under normal conditions, with a single monetary policy, it is the banks' quality and quantity of credit that determine the financial conditions for a large part of the productive fabric. The fact that the banking system was affected by serious difficulties indicates a credit role in holding back the modernization of the country. Bipop, Popolare di Novara, Banco di Napoli, Banco di Sicilia, Sicilcassa, CaRiPuglia, CaRiCal, CaRiVenezia, Banco Popolare di Lodi and many other smaller banks showed that the financial system had not been able to benefit from overall protected conditions. Almost fifteen years after the opening of the capital markets, the condition of the Italian banking market remained backward. Italian banks were fragmented and small; they had left many wholesale segments to foreign banks, limiting their activities to the retail network of not always transparent products, those distributed to savers at a high price.[11]

The backwardness of Italian banks will paradoxically prove to be a positive factor when the highly leveraged speculations of banks from other countries will bring the whole world to the brink of collapse. The banking channel is still the main method of financing for Italian companies; in several cases major business groups have been assisted by banks with the alleged aim of safeguarding the "system." An increasing number of firms participated in the equity capital of the banks, which in turn helped to perpetuate the control of industrial groups. The stock market was busier in monetizing minority holdings than in expanding existing businesses. Furthermore, non-bank credit (corporate bonds, securitizations or credit derivatives) was held back by abuse and sometimes outright scandal. All in all, the capital markets remained underdeveloped, despite Italy's stock of financial wealth being among the highest in the world in relation to its GDP. Indeed, because of this hidden trove in 2004 foreign banks became highly interested in Italian banks. Once more, the response of the Italian institutions took forms that resulted in the intervention of the judiciary, which contested the unscrupulous behavior of the directors of various banks.

Every year's Final Considerations of the Governor of the Bank of Italy presented on May 31 is the closest thing to a layman's version of a pope's prayer for the nation. All the important business leaders are summoned to the largest hall of Palazzo Koch, seat of Italy's central bank in the center of Rome. National broadcasting services show the governor's speech in real-time. In May 2006, the new governor of the Bank of Italy, Mario Draghi, opened his Final Considerations with explicit words: "With the end of last year, a convulsive period of scandals, of speculation, during which it seemed that the market, the savings of Italians, the destiny of companies in sectors relevant to the national economy were prey to the arbitrariness, the interest, the plots of a few individuals. The initiative of the judiciary prevented the completion of these plots ..." (Bank of Italy 2006).

5.8 As Stable as Germany

While the process of restructuring the industrial and financial system was underway, an unusual optimism spread about whether European rules would stabilize Italian public finances. Between the peak of 1994–1995 (127 percent) and 2007, the Italian public debt had dropped by about 27 points of GDP, falling slightly below 100 percent.

The decrease in debt was attributable to one-off tax revenues deriving from privatizations and the decline in the cost of the debt. Public spending had continued to increase even when the efforts to correct public finances had been most intense and the increase had only been offset by higher tax revenues.

Budgetary policy for the period from 1995 to 2007 must, however, be divided into two parts. Between 1995 and 2000, governments managed to obtain primary budget surpluses on average equal to 4.7 percent of GDP. Over the next six years, between 2001 and 2006, the primary surplus dropped on average to only 1.3 percent. Following France and Germany's violation of budgetary rules in 2003, the primary surplus in Italy fell to zero without raising eyebrows at the EU Commission.[12] Only in 2007, under the direction of Finance Minister Tommaso Padoa-Schioppa, did the budget surplus rise significantly, but once again through increases in the tax levy (2.8 percentage points of GDP between 2005 and 2007). Interestingly, the tax increase coincided with a growing number of firms turning to the "illegal or unobserved economy." The incidence of tax revenues on GDP climbed to 43.3 percent of GDP in 2007, just below the highest peacetime record of 1997, at the peak of the effort to meet the Maastricht criteria. It was almost 3 points higher than the average of the other EU countries. In ten years, the debt had therefore fallen but only through a tax burden that was unbearable and unpopular for honest taxpayers.

The change to a less ambitious fiscal policy after 2000 was due to several factors: Governments hoped for an "easier" phase with low-interest rates and monetary stability that made fiscal restrictions feel less necessary; and the elections showed considerable "fiscal fatigue" in the electorate, after a tax increase of 23 percent of GDP between 1992 and 2000. One reason, however, was the poor understanding of the country's conditions in the global and European context. Anti-European political attitudes on the part of the Berlusconi government paved the way for self-victimizing rhetoric concerning the "sacrifices imposed by Brussels." The anti-European attitude became a new hallmark of Italy's political–institutional uncertainty. After 2003, the government seized the opportunity offered by the fiscal overruns in France

General Government Gross Debt (% of GDP): the missed opportunity

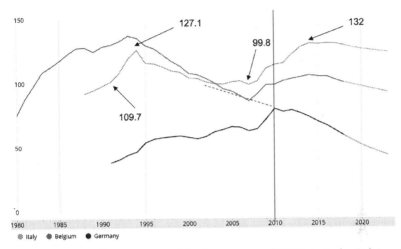

Figure 5.3 General government debt (percentage of GDP) in Italy, Belgium and Germany
Source: Data from IMF World Economic Outook

and Germany to ease spending. The primary surplus thus fell from 4.8 percent in 2000 to 0.3 percent in 2005.

The discontinuation in the reduction of public debt in the early 2000s was a fatal mistake. If, after 2001, governments had maintained the same primary surplus level as in the years 1995–2000, by 2008 the debt-to-GDP ratio would have dropped to between 80 percent and 85 percent of GDP (Fig. 5.3).[13]

In such circumstances, Italy would have faced the global and the European crises with the same level of debt-to-GDP as Germany, the same average growth rate as Germany in the precrisis decade, an industrial system less efficient and less productive than the German one, but with a less reckless banking system than the German one. Italy would therefore have been a "safe haven" during the global crisis and the successive euro crisis and would have attracted capital, as happened to Germany, which, without fiscal efforts, managed to bring the debt-to-GDP ratio below 60 percent in 2019.

In retrospect, it can be said that Italy's fiscal policy choices in the first decade of the twenty-first century amounted to the most damaging economic policy mistake in recent history. What emerges from the data for the period 2002–2006 is not so much a mistake in setting budget-ary policy objectives and in designing economic policies consistent with those objectives.[14] The real mistake was the regular overestimation of the future growth rate of the economy. Budgetary policy objectives were rigorous but based on excessively optimistic forecasts of eco-nomic conditions. In none of the years considered did the actual growth of the economy even come close to the one planned at the time the budget law was drafted. On average, each budget program esti-mated real economic growth of 2–3 points of GDP higher than the one subsequently achieved. Errors of this proportion are unique in the European panorama. Only two other countries have been identified by the European Central Bank as equally prone to erroneous forecasts on the fundamental variables of the economy: Greece and Portugal.

Was this a consequence of Berlusconi's archetypal belief in self-fulfilling optimism? Possibly, but what was observable were other fea-tures of "populist economics," such as short-termism: Not enough public resources were used in public investment, education, research and infrastructure, resources that could improve the transfer of skills from lagging to leading companies. Current expenditure continued to rise, hiding the problems of laggard regions and several sectors losing traction. As a result, pensions, social benefits and public administration expenses became increasingly difficult to reduce. The growth rate did not pick up and the tax burden grew, holding back private investments.

In those years, for the second time after 1992, the specific risk that made Italy's economic history a cautionary tale for other advanced democracies became tangible: a vicious circle set in between political uncertainty, a high level of public debt, a heavy tax levy and a damper on total investments, particularly those in "intangibles" such as soft-ware or research, which were critical for the country's productivity growth. Having failed to reach a lower level of debt, Italy found itself exposed to recessions and financial crises without the necessary man-euvering room to counter the fall of income or ensure the banking system's safety. The vicious circle would fully manifest itself after the global and European crises of 2008–2011, when in just a few years the country's history changed dramatically.

6 | *Sliding toward Zero Growth*

6.1 Years of Crisis, 2008–2013

For the Italian economy, the twin crises of 2008–2009 and 2011–2013 were the worst in peacetime history (Fig. 6.1). As we have seen, between 1929 and 1930 Italy's GDP declined by 6 percent and only in 1934 returned to its pre-crisis level. In comparison, between 2007 and 2010, GDP decreased by 6.5 percent, recovered slightly in the following two years and lost another 4.5 percent between 2011 and 2013, returning to the level of 2000. From 2007 to 2013, industrial production fell by almost a quarter and investments by as much as 30 percent. Private consumption shifted back to the levels of one generation earlier. The recession had a heavy impact on the number of employees and therefore on household incomes. Between 2007 and 2013, employment fell by over one million people, almost entirely in industry. Within a few years, the unemployment rate more than doubled from the lows reached in 2007.

The recovery from the 2007 crisis was slower not only than that of the 1930s but also, from the deep World War II income loss; and its long-term impact lasted longer than in any other previous economic crisis. At the end of 2019, before the pandemic crisis, Italian GDP was still more than 4 percent lower than in 2007. The impact on the growth trend was even more severe (Fig. 6.2). In the same period, the euro-area aggregate income level (excluding Italy) had exceeded the pre-crisis level by 15 percent. In 2007, the Italian economy made up 17.3 percent of the euro-area economy, in 2019 it represented only 15 percent.

The first 2008–2010 crisis hit a weak Italy without ammunition for defense. As already mentioned, the government budget had no room for maneuver to counter the recession or to consolidate the banking system.[1] However, Italy's vulnerability manifested itself with particular severity in the second crisis, triggered in mid-2011. In the summer of that year, Italian industrial production was still 15 percent below the

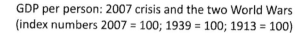

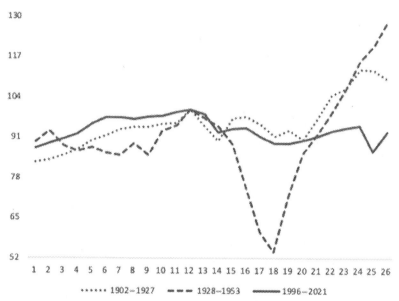

Figure 6.1 GDP per person during the 2008 crisis and the two World Wars
Source: De Nardis – Luiss-SEP

pre-2008 levels, while Germany had largely recovered the lost ground. German exports had already returned to 2007 volumes, while Italian exports were still 5 percent lower. In November 2011 the economy entered a recession. At the beginning of 2012, a 1.5 percent decline in GDP was forecast for 2012–2013, while *ex post* GDP shrank by 4.5 percent. Several factors intertwined and reinforced each other: the post-2011 drop in investment, the deceleration of international trade, the collapse of confidence in the euro-area outlook and the effects of the credit crunch and fiscal correction needed to save the country from a default that seemed imminent in the fall of 2011.

In a medium-term perspective, the most serious consequence of the crisis was perhaps the interruption of the reorganization and digitization undertaken by Italian companies since the launch of the euro, which, in 2007, promised to finally involve the whole productive system. A significant number of Italian companies had borrowed

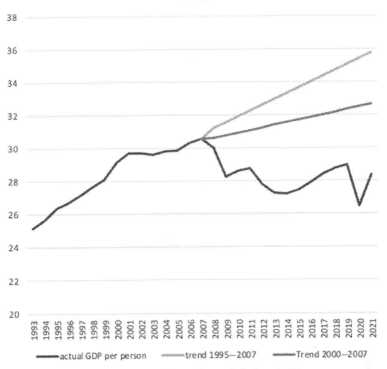

GDP per person - constant prices
€000s per person

Figure 6.2 Actual GDP per person and trends before 2007
Source: De Nardis – SEP-Luiss

heavily before the crisis precisely to increase their size and face the new global markets as best they could, or to acquire up-to-date technology, filling the technology gap accumulated since the 1990s. Suddenly this group, estimated at around 6,000 companies employing nearly a million workers, found it hard to access capital markets and bank financing.[2] Credit conditions became even more stringent due to the repercussions on bank balance sheets and the markets' distrust of the stability of European sovereign debts. The initial response to the global crisis by the banks was in fact to stop lending to non-financial companies whose growth died down in the six months after the Lehman Brothers' collapse. Loans and mortgages to households also suffered. The entire Italian economy went through a kind of financial asphyxiation. The cause was not only the decline in demand but a restriction on the supply of credit by the banks.

The fact that Italian banks were not significantly exposed to dangerous financial products, such as those that had caused the crisis in America, the UK, the Netherlands, Germany, France and Belgium, legitimated the idea that the Italian system was a fundamentally sound brokerage model, supported by a particularly prudent regulatory framework and supervision. While in other countries the taxpayers carried the consequences of the huge costs of bank bailouts, in Italy the belief was that it was not necessary to intervene with state money.

It subsequently turned out, however, that the balance sheet data of the Italian banks were not in as good a shape as they had been supposed to be. The average credit portfolio was quite risky, with non-performing assets higher than the European average; and profits had already been contracting in 2008, with a sharp decline in the return on capital and reserves. Years of generous credit to unprofitable clients, sometimes following a logic of bank–client connivance, had burdened bank balance sheets, making it more difficult to take on new risks or absorb losses when the economy needed them most. Year after year the denial of the banks' problems contributed to postponing the recovery. In hindsight, from the beginning of the millennium, economic policy has been framed in a very short forecasting horizon by political decision-makers and a policy framework based on the emergency idea of maintaining the waterline rather than undertaking navigation. While in 2008–2009 companies feared the future so much as to drastically cut planned investments, with a double-digit decline, banks and the government shared the forecast that in the space of a few months or perhaps a year the global crisis, which had suddenly come from the outside, would have disappeared just as quickly as it had arrived.

One of the fundamental reasons behind the short-termism of Italian governments is to be found in the size of the public debt. Any reform, as well as any investment beyond the short term, appeared to be unbearably risky, because a small decrease in GDP growth or tax revenue was believed to put debt refinancing at risk.

Short-termism remained a persistent factor, detaching political rhetoric from reality: No matter how many economic promises, no matter how many identity or ideological visions governments could offer to citizens, their room for maneuver was limited by short-run considerations on fiscal stability. The resulting disconnection between words and reality made citizens either credulous or completely skeptical of public powers, leaving unguarded the intermediate terrain of rational criticism, which must seriously take both words and deeds.

Among the unsolved problems in the years of rapid income growth stands out the completion of a modern welfare state, with universalistic coverage and social safety nets adequate to face severe crises. In 2009, only one in ten full-time workers in the private sector was entitled to an unemployment allowance of less than €500 per month. Such a thin safety net heightened the concern of families who reduced consumption with further depressive consequences on the economy. After declining since the beginning of the twenty-first century, both the number of poor and that of people at risk of poverty sharply increased during the crisis. The poverty gap widened between the country's North and South (Vecchi 2017: 444–449). The need to find employment of any kind pushed workers – and the productive system – to the lower ranks of productive jobs often through precarious short-term contracts. Young people were the harshest hit. In 2009, unemployment in the 20–34 age group reached 13 percent. In 2008–2014, the reduction in employment among young people was almost seven times greater than among the elderly.

Between 2007 and 2012, income fell by 10 percentage points in the South, against a decline of 4 points in the Center–North. In the South, the share of employed persons in the total active population fell further, against a slight increase in the North. Ten years after the beginning of the crisis, unemployment was still 18 percent higher in the South, compared to 7 percent in the Center–North.

6.2 Collapse of the Sovereign Debt

Between 2008 and 2010, the Italian government's main concern was to minimize the risk of its high debt being targeted by the financial markets. Once more, public debt vulnerability caused immobility and uncertainty. The clamorous falsification of Greece's financial accounts had brought the sustainability of the debt of various countries back into the market's crosshairs. The lack of fiscal room for maneuver made any form of perceived financial fragility riskier. While the Netherlands and Germany, thanks to their low public debts, managed to bail out their bankrupt banking systems using public resources, other countries were not able to do so because their debt was already too high.

Since the height of the Greek crisis in May 2010 European institutions, primarily the task force launched by President of the European
Council Herman van Rompuy, have interpreted the fragility of the
euro area as a fiscal problem, a consequence of overly high debts or
deficits in some countries. The signature of Italian Minister of Finance
Giulio Tremonti on the task force document – the basis and inspiration
for the management of the European crisis in the following years –
confirmed Italy's adherence to Europe's rigorist line.

In May 2010, the bailout of Greece was carried out by the European
Central Bank purchasing Greek government securities. The involvement of the ECB – so controversial as to cause a serious fracture within
its board – prompted its president, Jean-Claude Trichet, to ask the
leaders of the member states to set up a common fund for the rescue of
countries in financial distress, thus taking on a role that should never
have belonged to the European Central Bank. At the same time, the
finance ministers of the euro area had to informally undertake to
convince their countries' banks not to dump on the market the securities the ECB was trying to buy and to keep them in their portfolios for
at least three years.

The agreement was immediately violated by the French and Dutch
banks, which in a few days sold as much as half of the critical stocks in
their portfolios. The German banks, whose representative was the
CEO of Deutsche Bank, Josef Ackermann, vehemently protested to
the German government, but was persuaded by Finance Minister
Wolfgang Schäuble to keep the securities as promised to other countries. However, when Chancellor Merkel and French President Nicolas
Sarkozy announced in Deauville at the end of 2010 that the securities
held by private investors would be subject to restructuring (i.e. loss of
value), bankers and investors rebelled and began to sell the government
bonds of the high-debt countries. The ECB remained the only buyer of
such securities.

Meanwhile, the EU heads of government delayed the establishment
of the bailout fund, eventually endowing it with insufficient resources
and thus violating the commitment made to the ECB in May 2010. In
March 2011, the ECB Council reacted with a secret vote in which it
approved the suspension of the purchase of bonds of governments in
crisis. Although unannounced and unpublished, within six to eight
weeks the decision became clear to investors who found no buyers in
the market for those bonds. At that point, with the bonds of Greece,

Ireland and Portugal becoming unsaleable, investors around the world began to sell assets with a comparable level of risk, in order to hedge their portfolios. Massive sales of Italian and Spanish government bonds began in May and June 2011. When European governments agreed on the criteria for restructuring the Greek debt in July, sales of Italian and Spanish bonds became unstoppable.

The sequel was characterized by new ECB financial interventions in favor of Italy (and Spain) based on "conditionalities" detailed in a letter co-signed by ECB president Trichet and by Bank of Italy Governor Draghi. The ECB, in fact, began to buy Italian bonds, but after two weeks the Berlusconi government's commitment to reform pensions and control spending was rejected by the governing parties in parliament. In those months, in parallel with difficult financial conditions symbolized by the increase in the spread between Italian and German bonds, there was a new resonating collapse in investments in Italy. After the fall of around 16 percent in 2009 alone, a new collapse of similar size occurred in the second half of 2011. The spiral of distrust, both inside and outside the country, became so deep that it convinced Berlusconi himself, who arrived at his last international summit in conditions of poor lucidity (Bastasin 2015), to resign as leader of the government in November 2011. In his place, the President of the Republic appointed the president of Bocconi University and former EU commissioner Mario Monti.

In the days when Mario Monti took over the government, the Italian economy had just entered a recession. Dozens of European Commission and ECB officials had already been in Rome for weeks. A loan attempt by the International Monetary Fund was undertaken at the G20 summit in Cannes. In the last months of the Berlusconi government, Italy was under the surveillance of the ECB, the European Commission and the IMF, the three components of the Troika. Monti instead assumed the responsibility of the government upon himself, dismissing what he called the "foreign podestà" (city mayor in fascist times) and obtaining an overwhelming majority from parliament. His program, however, was largely already written, as he had to respect the commitments made by the previous government (starting with those indicated in 2010 by the task forces of the European Council and the Commission and then formulated in other Community forums, as well as in the ECB letter of August 2011 to which the Berlusconi government, unlike the Spanish one, had responded with total approval).

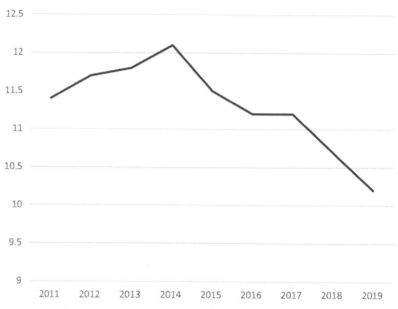

Figure 6.3 Share on GDP of the unobserved economy, 2011–2019
Source: Ministero dell'Economia e Finanza

Within a few weeks, the Italian Parliament approved severe pension reforms, taxation on primary residences and tough action to combat tax evasion. It succeeded in reducing the unobserved black economy (Fig. 6.3).[3]

The government then touched three sensitive nerves, all part of an "immoral" contract which had lasted for sixty years between an inefficient state and distrustful citizens: the pension promise, which the citizens themselves knew was unsustainable; the consequent investment of personal savings in real estate; and tolerated tax evasion. Despite the great consensus for Monti at the beginning of his mandate, it took only a few months for the populist parties that had brought Italy to the brink to relaunch themselves as defenders of the citizenry in the face of the severity of the sacrifices imposed by the Bocconi professor.

6.3 The Specter of Zero Growth

Despite the difficulties caused by a recession three times deeper than expected, the Monti government marked a philosophy change in the management of the country. From the end of 2011, the country engaged in extensive structural reform activity. Its aims and priorities were to create conditions conducive to growth rather than to distribute available resources. From the Monti government onward, interventions were launched to increase the efficiency of both labor and capital markets. With the social security reform of June 2012, a difficult reorganization of the main labor market institutions began, increasing the degree of flexibility in the use of the workforce and pursuing a more homogeneous distribution in terms of employment protection and access to social safety nets. Subsequently, labor contracts and training obligations were simplified, for the benefit of employers. In 2013, provisions were introduced aimed at improving the framework conditions for business activity. Other reforms made it easier for companies to have recourse to equity capital and encouraged investments in venture capital funds and in the venture capital of start-ups.

But the change of approach of the Monti government concerned a particularly new aspect in Italian economic policy, characterized by what we have defined as "partisan protectionism": Monti undertook reform policies that ran against both the Right and Left constituencies at the same time. After reforming the labor market, measures were adopted to make the capital of private enterprises more contestable and to stimulate business activity by increasing the level of competition, particularly in the professional service sector and in the network services complex, including transport, energy and communications. The process was continued by the next government, led by Enrico Letta. The reforms accelerated again in the first years of the Renzi government with the approval of a "Jobs Act," which further accentuated flexibility in the use of labor, but also introduced a single labor contract increasing workers' protections, created a national agency for employment and improved unemployment allowances.

Though incisive, these reforms were not enough to change the country's investment prospects (Fig. 6.4). In the absence of the financial stability provided by a European solidarity framework. The risk of financial instability linked to the high level of Italy's public debt, which had skirted the default risk in 2011, was still substantial.[4] Without Mario Draghi's "whatever it takes" magic trick, the Italian economy might have been crushed under the weight of its public debt instability.

Despite the efforts, the Italian economy was unable to fully recover from the shocks it suffered between 2008 and 2012. In the period after

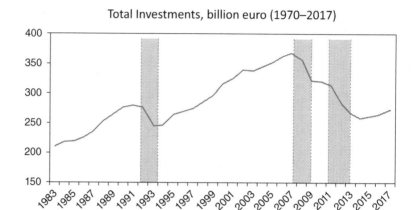

Note: grey zones identify phases of financial instability.

Figure 6.4 Gross capital formation, billion-euro, 2015 constant prices (1983–2017)

Source: Bastasin-Mischitelli-Toniolo "Living with high public debt – Italy 1861–2018" LUISS working paper 11/2019

2007, capital investments fell compared to the euro-area average specifically in the most important sectors: machinery and intellectual property (PRI) products, which include research and development and software. Investments in PRI were 2 percent higher in 2015 than in 2007. In the other European countries, however, the increase was ten times higher. After 2014, the contribution of capital per worked hour to labor productivity became negative, a result never previously recorded in Italian economic history, mainly due to tangible capital, while the contribution of intangible capital and ICT had fallen close to zero (Fig. 6.5).

GDP growth seemed to pick up in 2017 when it reached 1.5 percent. In large part, however, growth derived from unusually supportive macroeconomic policies: European monetary management was exceptionally favorable to the reduction of the Italian government bonds spread and budgetary policy was less restrictive than normal. The objective of the Renzi-Padoan government was to exploit the truce guaranteed by the ECB to hearten the economy. Investments increased by 3.8 percent in one year, although still very far from pre-crisis levels. However, the Italian system was not capable of self-sustainment. This became clear at the end of 2017 when the uncertainty over the political

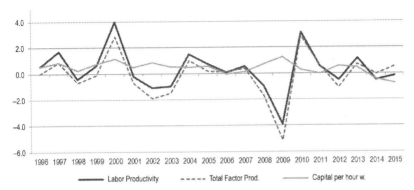

Figure 6.5 Labor productivity, TFP and capital per hour: Contribution to the growth of the economy 1995–2015
Source: ISTAT: "Le previsioni per l'economia italiana nel 2016" – Istat, Rome

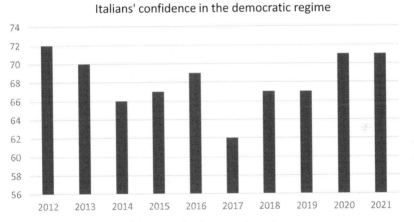

Figure 6.6 Italians' confidence in the democratic regime
Source: Demos "Rapporto gli italiani e lo Stato – 2021" – www.demos.it

scenario – accentuated by the failure of a constitutional referendum – was reflected once more in the fall in confidence in the democratic regime (Fig. 6.6).

Ten years after the global crisis, Italy's fragility was far from disappearing. The crisis had been too deep and long not to leave serious consequences: a lower endowment of capital, unused productive capacity and a high and prolonged level of unemployment that hindered the reintegration of many workers. Even in the year in

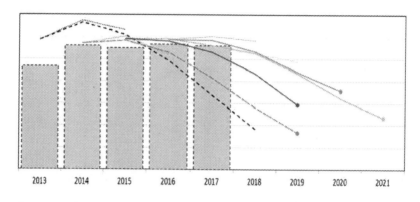

Governments between 2013 and 2017
Letta   -------------
Renzi   ....
Renzi   ───────────────
Renzi   ───────────────
Gentiloni   ....

Figure 6.7 Fiscal targets: Projections and realizations 2013–2021
Source: Authors' own elaboration

which the recovery was stronger, in 2017, the dynamics of labor productivity were less than half that of the rest of the euro area. Mistrust in the future of the country remained latent, in a context of fierce political antagonism. Excessive polarization was detrimental to the reputation of the democratic regime in the eyes of the electors (Fig. 6.6). Political fighting is also likely to impact the sentiment of confidence and stability coveted by potential investors. Between 2012 and 2017 Italy changed four different heads of government (Monti, Letta, Renzi and Gentiloni). Three of them lasted a few months. What emerged, however, was that the Renzi government, which lasted the longest, did not contribute to increasing the stability of the economic-policy action. On the contrary, just as with the two Berlusconi governments at the beginning of the century, the longer the government lasted, the weaker the fiscal action and the implementation of reforms became. This would dramatically confute the standard assumption that Italy's economic problems are mainly the result of political instability. Figure 6.7 shows how, after the first year, the Renzi government adopted a less consistent fiscal stance compared to the governments led by Letta and Gentiloni, each lasting about one year only.

This finding is likely to denote a structural character in Italian politics that refutes the internalization of fiscal discipline and reforms, which on the contrary are enforced in the first year by all governments in a need to consolidate their reputation under the pressure of the financial markets.

Without explicitly internalizing Italy's need for fiscal rebalancing, politics appears to be dependent on financial markets. Political actions are either frustrated or subject to a "Ricardian" response by the citizens who take fiscal stimulus as a premonition for tax increases down the road. Year after year, the electorate develops a skeptical attitude to which promises appear vain or false. Political credibility is regularly eroded.

In 2018, two parties capitalized on the feeling of mistrust and the sense of decline. Reflecting two different electoral bases, one in the North and the other in the South, the League and the Five Star Movement joined forces after the elections of March 2018, obtaining the majority of the parliamentary seats and assigning the leadership of the government to an inexperienced and little-known lawyer, Giuseppe Conte. The demands of the two parties were intended to materially please their respective electorates: a "citizenship income," helping the unemployed mostly in the South, and the reform of the 2012 pension reform ("quota 100"), favoring aged workers mostly in the North. The two reforms did not increase the labor input in the economy but rather reduced it. The two self-declared "populist" parties also shared a common protectionist sentiment. The League and the Five Star Movement were both tempted to return to the lira, revealed by the publication of a clumsy "Plan B" for the exit from the euro, written by a minister and some government advisers in May 2018, which caused a brutal halt in the arduous path of recovering the pre-2008 crisis investment level. Once more, the mechanism that linked institutional uncertainty, public debt instability and lower investments kicked in. The gap between the Italian and German long-term interest rates widened rapidly in 2018 when the populist government was instituted (Fig. 6.8).

In 2019, after the populist coalition broke up, the new government committed to a more stable agenda. The economy, however, remained stagnant. The level of investments was lower than in other comparable countries: While investment-to-GDP was 23 percent in France and 22 percent in Germany, it was only 17 percent in Italy and the quality

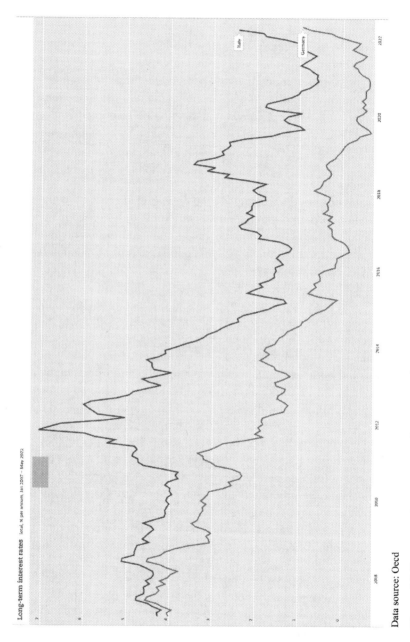

Long-term interest rates total, % per annum, Jan 2007 – May 2022

Data source: Oecd

Figure 6.8 Long-term interest rates: Germany and Italy 2007–2022
Source: OECD

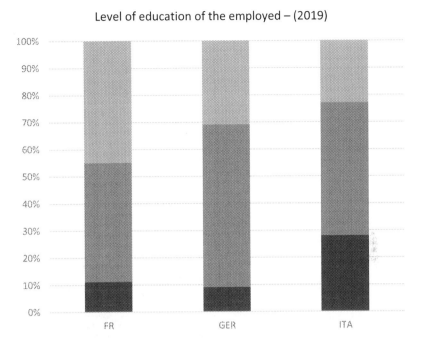

Figure 6.9 Share of highly educated workers: Italy, Germany, France
Source: ISTAT   www.istat.it/it/files//2021/12/Prospettive-economia-italiana_2021_
2022.pdf

of the production processes was aligned with the low share of highly educated workers in Italy's labor force (Fig. 6.9).

After 160 years, the Italian economy was reaching a level of potential growth close to zero (Fig. 6.10). In this perspective, the Italian case is truly unique because it raises questions that no other advanced economy has had to respond to yet: What happens when potential growth reaches zero? At what level should interest rates fall? And in the case of negative growth, is there any primary surplus that does not lead to a further fall in income and therefore an increase in debt in a vicious circle? These seem to be trivial questions, to which answers must already exist, but this is not the case because there have never been advanced countries whose potential growth has fallen to zero or negative levels.

As we noted several times, since Italy's unification in 1861 the country's economy has remained connotated by deep internal divisions, mostly among different geographical areas. Post-2008 Italian

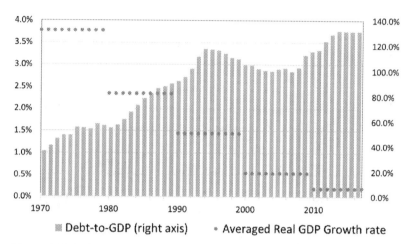

Debt-to-GDP (right axis)   **Averaged Real GDP Growth rate**

Figure 6.10 Debt-to-GDP and real GDP growth 1970–2017
Source: Bastasin-Mischitelli-Toniolo "Living with high public debt – Italy 1861–2018"
LUISS working paper 11/2019

stagnant economy added two political questions to the internal dila-
cerations: How can a democracy remain solid and peaceful when
economic growth slides to zero and someone's increase in income must
be mirrored by the loss of income of some other member of society? Is
a zero-growth or a negative-growth society destined to be ruled by a
non-democratic government?

These issues became extremely topical in February 2020, with the
outbreak of the pandemic crisis. Italy was hit earlier and harder than
any other non-Asian country by the sudden spread of the Coronavirus.
Drastic measures limiting the freedom of circulation and contact
among people had to be introduced. The economic consequences could
have been as catastrophic as the human toll. It was in this hardest
moment that the European Union reconstructed its solidarity. The ECB
contrasted the risk of market fragmentation with loose monetary
policies, both ordinary and extraordinary. The European
Commission designed, and the Council approved, the Recovery and
Resilience Facility, a special fund that provides vulnerable countries
with enormous financial assistance. The new facility was to be funded
through common resources and mutual debt. A new institutional
setting was to guarantee aid to those in need. Around one-third of
the total fund was destined for Italy. A special agreement between the
Italian government and the European institutions designed a sequence

of reforms that would be pre-conditional for the delivery of almost €200bn (11 percent of Italy's GDP) between 2021 and 2026.

Since the World War II Italy has never enjoyed what was normal elsewhere: a stable five-year program for reforming its economy. For the previous thirty years, the country never had fiscal margins remotely comparable to the resources made available by its European partners with the Recovery and Resilience Facility. Needless to say, the outcome of this unprecedented experiment in solidarity and reform is of such importance that it will define the future of Italy and of the European Union itself. It will also give special significance to the whole story of the Italian economy – between institutional fragility and personal vitalism – from 1861 until today.

7 | *The Canary in the Coalmine*

Italy's downhill turnaround has no precedent among advanced economies. At the beginning of 2022, per capita income of Italians was about 7 percent lower than in 2007. It corresponded to just over half of that of the United States, compared to about 70 percent in 1995–2000 (Table 1.2) when, at the height of a century-old process of convergence, labor productivity in Italy was at the level of the United States. In a quarter of a century, the per capita income gap between Italy and the most technologically advanced countries returned to the level of 1950, nullifying the catch-up between 1950 and 1995.

The link between economic decline and personal predicaments, both at an individual-psychological level and at a collective-political level, was very strong. When the economic decline began in 1995, so did the demographic decline. Twenty-seven years later, in 2022, deaths were double the births and the average age of Italians exceeded forty-six years. One in four Italians was over sixty-five years old. The fertility rate dropped to 1.24 children per woman, threatening a vicious circle of depopulation. Economic hardships influenced the individual choice of the young. Since the late 1990s, hundreds of thousands of well-educated young Italians have moved abroad searching for better job opportunities. In the South, among those who did not migrate, one in four chose not to study after the age of thirteen. In 2022, while schools and universities in Milan excelled, in the suburbs of Naples the percentage of students abandoning after lower education was close to 60 percent. The economic decline and the internal divergences were part of the citizens' daily experience and reverberated on the quality of Italy's political and social life, and even of its democracy.

This short history of the Italian economy began by recalling another episode of decline. Around 1500, the central and northern parts of the Italian peninsula enjoyed the highest per capita income in Europe. It then fell into a long era of stagnation during which the average living conditions of its inhabitants did not improve and probably diminished.

By the time of Italy's unification, the country that had been at the heart of the Renaissance had become one of the poorest and least educated in Western Europe. As we have seen, the process of unification into a single sovereign state was not easy: Growth accelerated in the early decades, but not enough to narrow the income gap with the major European countries. In 1893–1894, Italy experienced "the darkest years of the new kingdom," a financial crisis which could have been traumatic, not only economically. Between 1896 and 1913, the newly created central bank played a crucial role in stabilizing the banking sector while the adoption of time-consistent, monetary and fiscal policies put the country on a catch-up growth path with the more developed countries.

In the following century, the Italian economy moved from the periphery to the economic center of Europe. In the 1980s, it enjoyed levels of income and well-being aligned with those of the European countries that had been much more developed at the end of the nineteenth century. Convergence was not the result of chance. Workers, businesses and Italian institutions proved capable of exploiting the initial disadvantages (or as some scholars put it, the "advantages of backwardness") and translating them into growth factors. Before World War I, the country shared in the benefits of the "first globalization." It did not succumb in the 1930s to the dramatic crises of the time. After World War II, a swift reconstruction was followed by an extraordinary Golden Age. Italy continued to grow faster than did the initially more "advanced" countries even after the shocks of the early 1970s.

Italy's secular growth created the basis of a solid economy. In 1975, Italy was asked to join the G7 group of the most developed countries. In hindsight, however, over this period of strong growth Italy missed several opportunities to mend its old social and institutional flaws: In the early 1990s, the per capita income gap between North and South of Italy was deeper than it had been in the 1970s; the distance in the educational levels from the most advanced countries remained significant; public administration was not known for its efficiency; the quality and stability of economic and political institutions did not match those of other advanced economies; Italy's capitalism remained "feudal," closed and opportunistic; and public debt – for a century and a half higher than in other European countries – had grown to a peacetime record. While not inconsistent with the catch-up growth of a backward economy, those flaws became severe drawbacks in an economy that had come close to the technology frontier. It is largely due to the persistence of those "old ills" that Italians had reasons to be discouraged as the economy in the nineties started losing ground to its European neighbors.

In the previous pages, however, we highlighted the dialectic tension between Italy's economic vitalism and the weakness of its political life. This century-old tension, spurring individual resilience and surprising economic reaction, has remained a persistent feature in large parts of the country. The long economic convergence with the income levels of other advanced societies sedimented a tangible and intangible heritage that could still form the foundation of an economic revival. The weakness of Italy's larger companies was partly compensated for by a layer of medium-sized firms in the manufacturing sector. Social organizations, and local cultures, somehow upheld the vitality of Italian individuals to produce, innovate, invest and export. A dynamic core of technology and organization was maintained, which, given favorable market conditions and more apt institutions, could create the basis for new development. The opportunity arose immediately after Italy joined the euro, in the first decade of the millennium, when a growing number of companies showed signs of renewed vitality. At that juncture, Italy came close to resuming its secular growth path. It may be plausibly argued that, had the fiscal consolidation of the previous years continued, Italy would have faced the global and European crises of 2007–2012 from the same strong position that Germany did. In other words, it would have become, perhaps for the first time in several centuries, a "safe haven" attracting human and financial resources to complete the process of economic and technological modernization that was gaining ground.

The subsequent events were different. The Great Recession and then the European crisis were the most severe in the history of the Italian economy. Not only did they close the window of opportunities created between 2000 and 2007 by Italy's participation in the euro; they also reopened the wounds that had been bleeding for years.

We have identified the great coinciding shocks of the 1989–1992 period as the moment when the dialectic tension between politics and the economy became most acute and Italy lost its economic growth potential. We have observed how some of the old unsolved flaws, which up to the 1980s were still compatible with growth, proved to be powerful obstacles in the new technological framework accompanied by a rapid integration of the world economy. We are convinced that a crucial role was played by a causality chain linking political and institutional uncertainty to the high level of public debt, and the latter to financial instability. We identified a correlation between the interest rate differentials (an indicator of Italy's relative risk vis-à-vis other European countries) and investments in intangibles (research and development, and digital technology). Thus, Italy missed the first train of investments in information technology precisely when the new paradigm was changing the face of the world economy. Since the mid-1990s Italy's productivity has stagnated and the Italian economy lost contact with other advanced economies.

As shown in the previous pages, after 1992, with each episode of heightened uncertainty, an increasingly unstable public debt reverberated on the whole financial system, and on credit provision. Investors reacted abruptly, strongly reducing their engagement in the country's economy to an elsewhere unmatched extent. Due to uncertainty, Italy's capital endowment diminished year after year, and its quality was depleted.

Uncertainty has particularly been poisonous for intangible investments – primarily information technology – typically profitable only in the medium to long term and not backed by solid collateral assets. On the one hand, Italy's productivity declined in relative terms, vis-à-vis other developed economies, drawing down GDP growth. On the other hand, the divergence between social groups, economic sectors and geographic areas, all backed by strong political constituencies, increased the rigidity of public expenditure, forcing the state to raise taxation levels or increase public debt, thereby further reducing the incentives to invest. The intertwined threads of this complex situation became heavy chains keeping back economic growth.

It is a common argument that Italians have only themselves to blame for the dismal state of their economy. This is always a strong argument, but it would be misleading not to consider the efforts conducted in the past thirty years. Figures 7.1 and 7.2 show that after joining the euro Italy implemented more promarket reforms than France and Germany. The tax-to-GDP ratio considerably increased. The number of hours worked per worker is today one of the highest among European countries. Fiscal policy also challenges conventional assumptions: Italy's average primary surpluses between 1995 and 2019 were

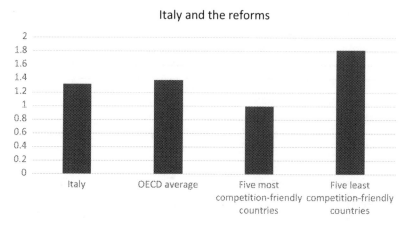

Figure 7.1 Italy and the reforms: OECD product market regulation indicators 2021

Source: OECD, Product market regulation indicators, Paris 2021

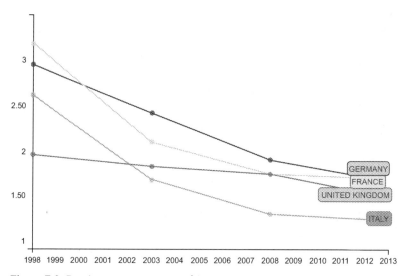

Figure 7.2 Barriers to entrepreneurship

Source: OECD, Product market Regulation Database

about 2.6 percent of Italy's GDP, which is five times higher than Germany's and twenty times higher than Ireland's, while for almost all the other European countries the average was negative. No other European citizens give to their state so much more than they receive in terms of public services. And yet, the chain of factors contributing to public debt vulnerability, economic uncertainty and political instability has remained strong.

It would thus be incorrect to say that, in the three decades of instability and relative impoverishment following the crisis of the early 1990s, Italians were not engaged in reforming the country's institutional and economic environment. Paradoxically, even changing the political majority at every electoral term could be interpreted as a relentless endeavor by the citizens to improve the situation. Some results of these efforts – although insufficient to reverse the course of the decline – were visible both in certain aspects of the economy and in the daily life of Italians. Large parts of the manufacturing sector successfully competed in the international markets. Between 2007 and 2021, Italian exports grew on average every year by 2.5 percent. From 2012 to 2021, the trade balance was always largely positive. Over the same period, while the share of Italy's GDP in the world economy declined to 1.9 percent, the Italian share in global trade remained constant at 2.9 percent. A sizable group of medium-sized enterprises thrived in international markets not only in the traditional "made in Italy" goods (fashion, food, leather, furniture) but also in advanced industries such as robotics (of which Italy is the sixth largest producer in the world). High-speed trains revolutionized intercity transport. Several city centers of high artistic value were revitalized. While the education gap with the rest of Europe remained wide, the share of people aged thirty to thirty-four with a university degree rose from 19.2 percent in 2008 to 27.8 percent in 2020 (ISTAT 2021: 3). Several museums have greatly improved their quality, organization and the number of visitors, also as a result of the employment of international managers and the relaxation of centralized red tape. In many of these and other cases, the ingenuity of some individuals, entrepreneurs, managers, teachers or city mayors, made up for a sometimes dysfunctional and mistrusted state. Even within the public sector, the dynamism and inventiveness of those in charge occasionally helped overcome bureaucratic inefficiency. These and several other instances go some way in showing the vitality of traditional Italian individualism and civil society. The century-old economic self-defense from the state has both good and bad – sometimes very bad – consequences. However, this social vitalism is an important, if not single, explanation of why Italy's economy and society did not succumb to the longest and most serious crises in its history, despite the loss of income, the doubling of the number of poor and, what possibly matters most for a satisfactory life, the sheer risk of falling into poverty.

Although economic vitality remained ingrained in large segments of Italian society, three decades of economic stagnation worsened the business conditions and finally morphed into deeper political instability. Even Italians' satisfaction with democracy became unsteady In this regard, the history of Italy's twenty-first century is a cautionary tale for other countries questioning the quality of their democracy or heading toward a slowdown in long-term growth. It may not be incidental that Italy's political experiences are replicating elsewhere: Political polarization is plaguing the USA; the regional dichotomy is opening more widely in Spain, France, Eastern Europe and the UK; political instability occurs in most of Europe – the duration of British premiers since 2007 is similar to that of Italy; and public debt in France or in the USA in 2020 was much higher than Italy's in 2008. Other, more subtle, analogies could be found, with Italy possibly playing the role of the canary in the coal mine of democracy.

According to the polls (Fig. 7.3), Italians are growing disenchanted with democracy, to the point that the majority of citizens believe that the democratic system cannot mend its own flaws. Italians' demand for radical political change, which does not necessarily coincide with a more democratic system, is arguably related to the economic predicaments that the last generations have experienced (Fig. 7.4). Italians seem to have lost faith in their state even more than in their governing elite, the latter often integrated by capable experts (Fig. 7.5). Italians' irritation toward politics and concern for the economy goes some way in explaining why they have embraced technocratic – or supra-national – solutions, after being tempted, and regularly disappointed, by populist leaders.

However, Italians' mistrust of the state and their loss of confidence in the improvement of public functions can be real problems in modern times. As mentioned in the introduction, in a system of global compe-tition, public powers are not irrelevant, and even a vibrant economy cannot flourish without the support of efficient public functions such as the provision of financial stability, welfare assistance, antitrust regula-tions, and well-functioning judicial and educational systems. Moreover, global competition requires an alignment of productivity and labor conditions, and the necessary labor flexibility is possible only

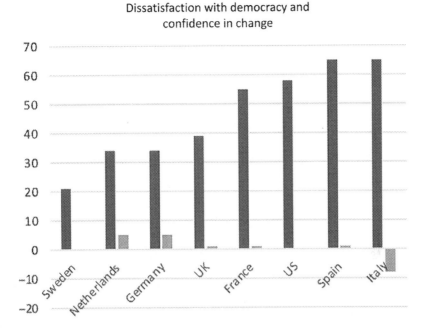

Figure 7.3 Dissatisfaction with democracy and confidence in change
Source: Authors' elaboration on Pew-research data

if a high level of decentralization allows salary and productivity to go hand in hand. However, we observed that weak, unstable or indebted central governments find it politically more difficult to afford a high degree of regional differentiation or decentralization. In this sense, a weak political system can contribute to the loss of productivity.

Democracies affected by wide internal fractures require the state to provide a stable framework. To do this, the state should deliver the protection of rights and guarantees of security to all individuals at an adequate level. This requires a protective state, a strong defense of the rule of law, a positive attitude toward new opportunities, and a society in which the individuals' freedom goes hand in hand with an adequate degree of responsibility for the rest of society. Since its unification, Italy has often resorted to public debt to try and make this complex set of values compatible with each other, even at times of high GDP growth.

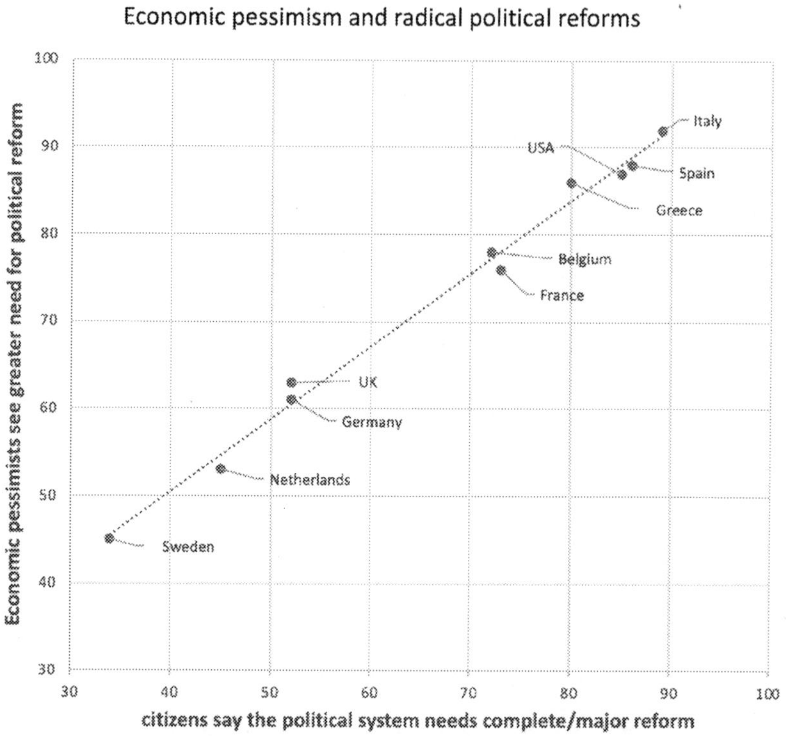

Economic pessimism and radical political reforms

Figure 7.4 Economic pessimism and request for radical political reforms
Source: Authors' elaboration on Pew-research data

Rather than echoing individual or social responsibility, public debt has crystallized social and structural backwardness, perpetuated bad politics and slowed down the growth of the economy.

After the capital market liberalization of the 1980s, the high level of public debt produced a latent risk of instability, feeding uncertainty about future interest rates and taxation levels as well as the margins available for macroeconomic stabilization policies in case of recessions.

We observed that investments in Italy fell by about 15 percent during any episode of financial instability: in 1992–1993, in 2008–2009 and in 2011–2012 (Fig. 6.4). Protracted episodes of falling investments reduce the quantity and the quality of capital endowment and, through various channels, reduce the level of growth of the economy until it reaches zero or becomes negative. At that point, an even more vigorous fiscal effort would be required to reduce the debt,

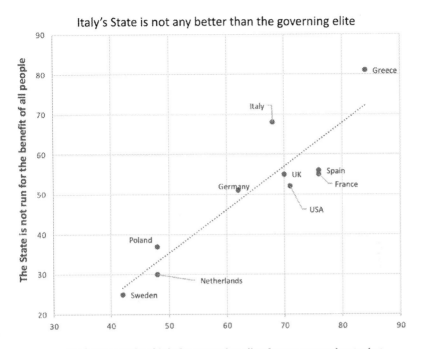

Figure 7.5 Confidence in the elites versus confidence in the state
Source: Authors' elaboration on Pew-research data

with the risk of political and economic backlashes. In other countries there was no lack of reasons for uncertainty but in none of them the instability was enhanced by too large a public debt, impacting the financial and banking system and the entire economy. Every shock, either external or internal, had repercussions on the whole structure of the Italian economy.

In the early 2020s, after decades of relative decline, the Italian economy came close to a condition of very low growth. Such a situation solicits a number of questions: Why would anyone invest in a country that, on average, cannot deliver positive returns on capital for the foreseeable future? How is it possible to reduce public debt when interest rates, however exceptionally low, cannot be lower than the growth rate of GDP? How can the country break the high debt–low growth vicious cycle? Shouldn't the debate between economists and politicians on "austerity" and fiscal stimulus be reviewed in the special case of a country no longer capable of growing? Finally, what resources could Italy mobilize?

Italian history shows that the country has already overcome very serious crises, which to many appeared as deadly challenges. The bankruptcy of the entire banking system in 1893–1894 was then followed by a phase of rapid growth; the country that in 1943–1945 was divided by a civil war was rapidly reconstructed economically, institutionally and civilly; the years of terrorism (1970s) were overcome with a united effort and, subsequently, a patient fight against inflation. On the other hand, it is worth recalling that the crisis of 1919–1922 was also overcome, but at the cost of sacrificing democracy for the sake of stability.

In Italy, episodes of recovery coincided with periods of political stability. The latter has functional relevance for the economy. However, under the special Italian circumstances of the first decades of the twenty-first century one could argue that it may even have been detrimental. Since the year 2000, contrary to the conventional understanding of Italy's problems, the longer the governments lasted the less they have committed to fiscal stabilization. What happened then may not be a conclusive demonstration, but it adds to the idea that something in Italy's political culture needs to be improved.

Italy's political and financial fragility casts a shadow on the country's solidity as a partner for the rest of Europe, especially in a historical phase requiring Europe to assume stronger and united responsibility in the face of wars, technological challenges, geopolitical tensions and global health crises. In the past, other European countries dismissed Italy for its cultural idiosyncrasies and used it as an alibi to avoid closer European cooperation.

Most recent events indicate that Italy's problems may indeed have a European solution. From the 1960s, as said above, a pattern emerged in which capital investments declined in Italy whenever institutional uncertainty was followed by financial instability. However, in February 2020 a deadly health crisis struck the world – and Italy was hit harder and earlier than most other advanced societies – without producing the usual collapse in investments. The pandemic might have buried the Italian economy for good, but on the contrary, investment recovery in Italy was stronger than in other European countries after the health shock.

Active macroeconomic intervention at the European level allowed
Italy's economy to recover most of its fall in GDP in less than two
years. The European framework – legal, administrative and financial –
and the availability of macroeconomic tools completely changed Italy's
consolidated pattern of the previous fifty years through institutional
stability, coordinated fiscal and monetary policies, financial solidarity
and political trust. The construction, manufacturing and banking
industries, tempered through decades of predicaments, responded vigorously, anticipating European stability and support. Not everything
worked well: Italy's public administration immediately appeared
unable to efficiently manage the 200 billion obtained by the
European Union. More importantly, Italy's public discourse ended
up neglecting the political significance of Europe's generosity, as it
was demonstrated by a real paradox: the electoral victory of a nation-
alist party in September 2022 in the moment when Europe was
granting huge and vital aid to the country.

What happened in the collaboration between Italy and its European
partners still requires a learning process and political acknowledgment
in Italy.

The post-pandemic European policies engaged common European
resources and entailed penetrant conditionality at the national level,
completely reversing the idea of exclusive national sovereignty on
money and even politics. In connection with Italy's economic history,
the European aid and conditionalities were beneficial for individuals'
economic vitalism, resolving, the centuries-old tension between the
economy and politics in Italy. That tension, grounded in the old-seated
problematic relationship between Italian citizens and their public
powers, is now expanding and reproducing through globalization –
and its lack of governance – for the citizens of most other countries.

In the context of the new interdependent world, Italians benefited
greatly from an institutional setting that went beyond that of the
national state. In times of misalignment between global challenges
and national politics, understanding the Italian historical experience
may have a relevant significance for other countries as well.

Notes

Chapter 1

1 The Venetians did not want to abandon the traditional flat keel design of their ships to adopt the Portuguese and Dutch model of vessels suitable for ocean navigation.
2 "Franza o Spagna, purché se magna."
3 Cassese, Sabino (2014) "Governare gli Italiani" Il Mulino (Bologna).
4 Research on income and wealth of Europe since the Middle Ages has made considerable progress in the last two decades (Forquet and Broadberry 2015). Maddison's estimates of historical GDP are now continued in Groeningen by The Maddison Project (2020). The latter, however, largely overstates Italy's GDP at the time of unification, relative not only to Maddison's own previous estimates but also to several other scholars and literary evidence.
5 The first law against child labor came out in 1843 in Lombardo-Veneto, but practices of underage employment were frequent in the South until the 1970s.
6 In Italian historiography, the 1848–1849 war between the Kingdom of Sardinia (which included Piedmont and was administered from Turin) and Austria is called the First Italian War of Independence.
7 Castellani (2009) is more optimistic in putting to 10 percent the share of the population capable of understanding and speaking a common language.
8 Daron Acemoglu, James A. Robinson. (2012) *Why Nations Fail: The Origins of Power, Prosperity, and Poverty*, New York: Crown Business.

Chapter 2

1 The Webster International Dictionary lists risorgimento as an English masculine noun meaning "a time of renewal or renaissance." In Italian it is the name given to the historical period for the struggle of independence and Italy's unity from its first movements (1820–1821, 1831) to the insurrections and wars of 1848–1866.
2 Ciocca (2007: 70).

3 Cotroneo G. and Quaglieni P. F. (eds.) (2011), Discorsi su Stato e Chiesa di Camillo Cavour, Rubbettino.

4 Letter of the President of the Federal Convention, dated September 17, 1787, to the President of Congress, Transmitting the Constitution.

5 Cassese, Sabino, "Governare gli Italiani."

6 Merchant Sebastiano Wagner and the engineer Francesco Varé.

7 This should not surprise today's European citizens, who see that there is still no complete banking union, a quarter of a century after the introduction of the euro.

Chapter 3

1 Vienna's splendor, however, was due much more to its being the capital of a large empire than by being an economy that was much livelier than Italy's.

2 According to the Statute (the Constitution of the Kingdom of Italy), "the State is governed by a monarchical-representative government" (art. 2). "The person of the king is sacred and inviolable" (art. 4). "The executive power belongs to the king alone" (art. 5). Foreign affairs and command of the armed forces are reserved for him. The king appoints the senators (art. 33), convenes the two chambers, and can extend, and dissolve the Chamber of deputies (art. 9). Of the eighty-four articles of the Statute, twenty-two ensure the preeminent position of the sovereign, and only eight are dedicated to regulating (but generically) the rights and freedoms of citizens. The judicial function is not attributed to the State, but to public officials with particular guarantees (immovability), whose careers largely depended on the executive power (minister of justice). In the Statute, there was no mention of the government. It only said that "the ministers are responsible" (art. 67), without indicating to whom.

3 This period included the fascist twenty years, during which, in 1928, the electoral body was called to approve just a list of names indicated by the Grand Council of Fascism. In 1939, the elections were suppressed.

4 The season in which "the triumph of the bourgeoisie" was celebrated had ended together with the belief in continuous progress. The liberal–bourgeois civilization was rejected because it was entrenched in forms of political socialization that were individualistic in mobilization and dialogic–rational in communication. Italy's political system was also not supported by a strong administrative structure, like those well established in France and the United Kingdom, and even more so in Germany. In the absence of strong social structures, mass society tends to be more exposed to emotional rhetoric, frequently tinged with anti-political overtones.

5 Cassese, ibid.

6 Exactly the opposite of what was done in the Giolitti era.
7 First published in 1947, the book was an immediate international success with translations in several languages; for a recent English edition, see Carlo Levi, *Christ Stopped at Eboli*, Macmillan, London 2021.
8 The multilateral payments system makes it more difficult to introduce protectionist retaliations against one country. While in case of conflictual relationships bilateral payments system are more vulnerable.
9 Carli, ibid.
10 Carli 1996: p. 151.
11 Carli, ibid., p. 165.
12 In 1966, a ruling of the Constitutional Court defined the indebtedness of the state in compliance with article 81 of the Constitution, which instead should have prevented recourse to public expenditure without financial coverage. The rationale was that the debt would allow for a future expansion of income in a logic of economic planning. The Court embraced the consensus of the time that Italy needed "yearly growth of at least 5 percent to compensate for social conflicts or regional and sectoral imbalances" (Carli, ibid.).

Chapter 4

1 Eurispes: https://eurispes.eu/news/eurispes-comunicato-ricerca-corruzione-tra-realta-e-rappresentazione/.
2 Italy results forty-fourth in the WEF competitiveness index (2021); fifty-eighth in the World Bank "Doing business" index; fifty-seventh in the Heritage Index of economic freedoms (between Panama and Armenia); sixty-third in the Global Gender Gap Index.
3 The three main Italian parties had collectively received 75 percent of the votes in the European elections of 1989.
4 A purely illustrative comparison between a stock (financial wealth) and a flow (GDP).
5 The currency crisis of 1992 demonstrated the unpreparedness of European countries in the face of an epochal change that occurred in the 1980s with growing international financial integration (Group of Ten, 1993). In 1986, the Single European Act prepared the launch of the capital market in 1990, but the overall volume of transactions in the main financial centers had tripled between 1986 and 1992. The goal of coordinating European economies was lagging behind the instability introduced by the enormous mobility of capital, by the spread of derivative financial instruments, in particular for hedging exchange risks, and by the automation of exchanges that allowed investors to change their behavior in a few moments. All this

made poorly coordinated responses by the political and monetary authorities of the various countries less effective than in the past.

6 According to Svimez data, in the period 1992–1997 consumption in the South increased on average by only 0.6 percent, while investments in public works suffered, between 1991 and 1997, a cumulative decline of 57 percent. In the absence of compensation from the private economy, the impact of the new public spending policies ended up decreeing two long-lasting consequences: the widening gap between the economic trends of the North and the South and the rigidity of public spending destined for backward regions.

7 The definition was first given by former Constitutional Court judge Sabino Cassese.

8 A more analytical assessment in Buiatti C., Carmeci G., Mauro L.: "The Origins of the Public Debt of Italy: Geographically dispersed Interests?" – *Journal of Policy Modeling* Volume 36, Issue 1, January–February 2014, Pages 43–62.

Chapter 5

1 Most firms acted cautiously, not through forms of direct investment, but through non-equity investment in joint ventures or through the purchase of patents.

2 Including Mediobanca which, due to lack of knowledge of the German market, had grossly mismanaged Pirelli's acquisition of the German tire producer Continental in the early 1990s.

3 At the beginning of the 1990s, IRI was the largest Italian industrial group with about 500 companies and 400,000 employees, but its financial condition was dramatic. It had debts of 82,000 billion lire and it was, once again, the European Commission at the end of 1993, fearing an insolvency crisis, to impose rules similar to those of "a prudent private investor."

4 The definition was coined by former prime minister Giuliano Amato.

5 This arranged for public credit institutions and savings banks to form joint-stock companies by conferring the capital to "Foundations of banking origin." The spirit of the reform was to gradually improve the degree of competition by assigning antitrust functions to the supervisory institution. The Foundations then had to sell the shares on the market, but they did so very gradually.

6 https://sep.luiss.it/sites/sep.luiss.it/files/PB11.22%20How%20Italy%20was%20about%20to%20be%20excluded%20from%20the%20euro.pdf.

7 The process put in place by the new global competition has been painful. However, starting from the mid-1990s, a core of about 3,700 medium-sized companies, which employed almost 500,000 workers, managed to increase turnover, support exports by specializing in market niches, develop research, connect manufacturing and services, and expand into international markets. To spread and consolidate, this fundamental creative phase would have required both an efficient capital market and appropriate corporate governance structures. Furthermore, an adequate degree of flexibility in the labor and capital markets, offset by social safety nets for those affected by lower job security, would have made it possible to shift human and financial resources toward companies capable of growth rather than anchoring them in those kept afloat only by subsidies and bank connections.

8 After suffering the partial detachment from the German industrial chains with the opening of the economies of Eastern Europe, Italy participated in the global value chains but remained halfway there: Labor costs in relation to productivity were too high to compete with emerging countries; the technological knowledge of companies and the workforce were too poor or unevenly distributed to participate in the global innovation cycle. Finally, business leaders were too insecure, or their firms' size too small, to lead the "chains" on a global scale. Furthermore, the impact of global trade organized according to value chains was dramatically differentiated within the country. The South benefited less than the North and the Center, not only in relations with international producers but also in participation in "interregional value chains" (Cherubini and Los 2016). Producers in Northern or Central Italy found it more convenient to turn to producers in Eastern Europe, or in the Balkan and Mediterranean areas, than to suppliers from the Southern regions.

9 When the Berlusconi government approved the Maroni law on the labor market – based on the White Paper of 2001 and moreover in some continuity with the Treu law of 1997 – the clash between companies and trade unions was so hard that it coincided with the return of terrorism and the killing of the labor-law scholar Marco Biagi.

10 N. 864 – La misurazione dell'economia sommersa attraverso l'approccio della domanda di circolante (solo in inglese): Una reinterpretazione della metodologia con un'applicazione all'Italia. Measuring the underground economy with the currency demand approach: A reinterpretation of the methodology, with an application to Italy.

11 Alessandro Penati: "La Questione Bancaria" – Banca, Impresa, Società (Il Mulino) August 2013.

12 The EU Commission did not raise objections to Italy's trajectory, which formally did not violate the numerical thresholds of the Growth and Stability Pact.

13 Our calculations take into account both the negative effect on the growth
    rate of the economy and the positive effect of attracting capital from the
    rest of the euro area.
14 https://sep.luiss.it/sites/sep.luiss.it/files/Living%20with%20high%
    20public%20debt%20-%20Bastasin.Mischitelli.Toniolo%20-WP.pdf.

Chapter 6

1 The global crisis of 2008 caught Italian companies in the middle of a
   transition and their reaction was immediately dramatic. The first to review
   their plans for the worse were the companies that had managed to engage
   in global trade and were more exposed to the international crisis. Cases of
   temporary closure of entire factories or production lines became numerous
   and happened in rapid succession. The new margins of labor flexibility
   allowed for the temporary reduction of the workforce, which, however, in
   some cases became permanent. It would be precisely the companies that
   made use of flexibility that would recover better, subsequently engaging
   the global recovery cycle. But the absence of adequate shock absorbers put
   the costs of the crisis on workers and their families.
   In a short time, the shocks – the rise in unemployment, the collapse of
   foreign trade and the financial heart attack – extended to domestic
   demand and therefore also to companies nestled in what they thought
   were protected domestic sectors. Within a few months of the collapse of
   Lehman Brothers, the hardest hit companies were those halfway along the
   value chain: Large companies were in fact able to postpone purchases of
   semi-finished products and capital goods and impose ever longer deferred
   payments to their suppliers. The latter saw their very survival at risk.
   Uncertainty about the future and the effect of lower foreign demand
   caused investments in the manufacturing sector to drop by 20 percent in
   the space of a few months.
2 Banks were paralyzed by bad debts; bankruptcy procedures and often
   opaque and continuous bureaucratic obstacles prevented many entrepreneurs from getting back on their feet.
3 For a discussion of methodology see Ardizzi et al. (2012).
4 The banking system remained vulnerable, burdened by an enormous
   amount of unsuccessful loans or risk, also demonstrated by cases of bad
   credit management that escaped supervision. The tax burden was still too
   burdensome and the efficiency delays that had accumulated in the public
   machinery, education, research and physical and intangible infrastructures
   for decades were still too heavy. After the crisis, the Italian economy still
   has not managed to embark on a path of strong and sustainable growth.

References

Abramovitz M., 1989, *Thinking about Growth and Other Essays on Economic Growth and Welfare*, Cambridge: Cambridge University Press.

Acemoglu D. and Robinson J. A., 2013, *Perché le nazioni falliscono*, Milan: Il Saggiatore.

Amatori F., Bugamelli M. and Colli A., 2013, "Technology, Firm Size, and Entrepreneurship," in Toniolo G. (ed.), *The Oxford Handbook of the Italian Economy since Unification*, Oxford and New York: Oxford University Press, pp. 455–485.

Angeloni I. and Gaiotti E., 1990, *Note sulla politica monetaria italiana negli anni Ottanta*, Rome: Bank of Italy.

Ardizzi G., Petraglia C., Piacenza M. and Turati G., 2012, Measuring the Underground Economy, with the Currency Demand Approach (Working Paper 864), Rome: Bank of Italy.

Baldini A. and Pellegrini G., 2017, "Prezzi e concorrenza," in Gigliobianco A. and Toniolo G. (eds.), *Concorrenza, mercato e crescita in Italia: il lungo periodo*, Venice: Marsilio, pp. 271–307.

Bank of Italy, 1980, 1993, 1995, *Considerazioni finali del Governatore*, Rome: Bank of Italy.

Barbiellini Amidei F., Cantwell J. and Spadavecchia A., 2013, "Innovation and Foreign Technology," in Toniolo G. (ed.), *The Oxford Handbook of the Italian Economy since Unification*, Oxford and New York: Oxford University Press, pp. 378–416.

Bastasin C., 2015, *Saving Europe: Anatomy of a Dream*, Washington, DC: Brookings Institution Press.
    2018, "*The Euro and the End of 20th Century Politics*," Rome: SEP-LUISS.

Bastasin C., Mischitelli M. and Toniolo G., 2019, "Living with High Public Debt, Italy 1861–2018," Rome: SEP-LUISS.

Bertola G. and Sestito P., 2013, "Human Capital," in Toniolo G. (ed.), *The Oxford Handbook of the Italian Economy since Unification*, Oxford and New York: Oxford University Press, pp. 249–270.

Bianco M. and Napolitano G., 2013, "Why the Italian Administrative System Is a Source of Competitive Disadvantage," in Toniolo G. (ed.), *The Oxford Handbook of the Italian Economy since Unification*, Oxford and New York: Oxford University Press, pp. 533–570.

Boltho A., 2013, "Italy, Germany and Japan: From Economic Miracles to Virtual Stagnation," in Toniolo G. (ed.), *The Oxford Handbook of the Italian Economy since Unification*, Oxford and New York: Oxford University Press, pp. 108–133.

Bonelli F., 1978, "Il capitalismo italiano, linee generali di interpretazione," in Romano R. and Vivanti C. (eds.), *Storia d'Italia: Annali Vol 1, Dal feudalesimo al capitalismo*, Turin: Einaudi, pp. 1193–1255.

Bosworth R., 1979, *Italy the Least of the Great Powers*, Cambridge: Cambridge University Press.

Brandolini A. and Bugamelli M., 2009, *Rapporto sulle tendenze nel sistema produttivo italiano*, Occasional Paper, April. Rome: Bank of Italy.

Broadberry S., 2016, "The Great Divergence in the World Economy: Long-Run Trends of Real Income," in Baten J. (ed.), *A History of the Global Economy: From 1500 to the Present*, Cambridge: Cambridge University Press, pp. 35–39.

Broadberry S., Giordano C. and Zollino F., 2013, "Productivity," in Toniolo G. (ed.) *The Oxford Handbook of the Italian Economy since Unification*, Oxford and New York: Oxford University Press, pp. 186–226.

Broadberry S. and Harrison M., 2005, "The Economics of World War I: An Overview," in Broadberry S. and Harrison M. (eds.), *The Economics of World War I*, Cambridge: Cambridge University Press, pp. 3–41.

Bugamelli M. and Pagano P., 2004, "Barriers to Investment in ICT," *Applied Economics*, 36 (20), pp. 2275–2286.

Calligaris S., Del Gatto M., Hassan F., Ottaviano G. and Schivardi F., 2018, "The Productivity Puzzle and Misallocation: An Italian Perspective," London: CEPR. (https://cepr.org/sites/default/files/events/papers/995_Productivity%20Puzzle%20and%20Misallocation.pdf.

Carli G., 1993, *Le due anime del Faust: Scritti di economia politica*, Rome: Laterza.

1996, Cinquant'anni di vita italiana, Rome: Laterza.

Cassese S., 2019, *Governare gli italiani: storia dello Stato*, Bologna: Il Mulino.

Castellani A., 2009, *Nuovi saggi di linguistica e filologia italiana e romanza (1976–2004)*, edited by Della Valle V. et al., Rome: Salerno.

Cavazzuti F., 2017, "Un racconto di economia sul protezionismo interno," in Gigliobianco A. and Toniolo G. (eds.), *Concorrenza, mercato e crescita in Italia: il lungo periodo*, Venice: Marsilio, pp. 451–490.

Cesarano F., Cifarelli G. and Toniolo G., 2012, "Exchange Rate Regimes and Reserve Policy: The Italian Lira 1883–1911," *Open Economies Review*, 23, pp. 253–275.

Cherubini L. and Los B., 2016, "Regional Employment Patterns in a Globalizing World: A Tale of Four Italies," in Cherubini L. and Los B. (eds.), *Global Value Chains: New Evidence and Implications* – Workshops and Conferences, Rome: Bank of Italy.

Chiarini R., 2021, *Storia dell'antipolitica italiana dall'Unità a oggi*, Soveria Mannelli: Rubbettino.

Ciocca P., 2007, *Ricchi per sempre? Una storia economica d'Italia (1796–2005)*, Turin: Bollati Boringhieri.

2014, *L'IRI nella economia italiana*, Rome: Laterza.

2018, *Tornare alla crescita: Perché l'economia italiana è in crisi e cosa fare per rifondarla*, Rome: Donzelli.

Cipolla C. M., 2013, *Uomini, tecniche, economie*, Bologna: Il Mulino.

Cotroneo G. and Quaglieni P. F. (eds.), 2011, *Discorsi su Stato e Chiesa di Camillo Cavour*, Cantanzaro: Rubbettino.

Crafts N., 2018, *Forging Ahead, Falling Behind, and Fighting Back: British Economic Growth from the Industrial Revolution to the Financial Crisis*, Cambridge: Cambridge University Press.

Crafts N. and Magnani M., 2013, "The Golden Age and the Second Globalization in Italy," in Toniolo G. (ed.), *The Oxford Handbook of the Italian Economy since Unification*, Oxford and New York: Oxford University Press, pp. 69–107.

Craveri M., 2016, *L'arte del non governo*, Venice: Marsilio.

Daniele V. and Malanima P., 2007, *Il divario Nord-Sud in Italia 1861–2011*, Catanzaro: Rubbettino.

De Martino P. and Vasta M. (eds.), 2018, *Ricchi per caso: La parabola dello sviluppo economico italiano*, Bologna: il Mulino.

De Mattia R., 1959, *L'unificazione monetaria italiana*, Turin: ILTE.

De Mauro T., 1963, *Storia linguistica dell'Italia unita*, Rome: Laterza.

Eichengreen B. and Uzan M., 1992, "The Marshall Plan: Economic Effects and Implications for Eastern Europe and the USSR," *Economic Policy*, 13, pp. 13–75.

Federico G. and Wolf N., 2013, "A Long-Run Perspective on Comparative Advantage," in Toniolo G. (ed.), *The Oxford Handbook of the Italian Economy since Unification*, Oxford and New York: Oxford University Press, pp. 327–350.

Feinstein C., 1995, *Banking, Currency and Finance in Europe between the Wars*, Oxford: Clarendon Press.

Felice E., 2013, *Perché il Sud è rimasto indietro*, Mulino, Bologna.

Fenoaltea S., 1983, "Italy," in O'Brien P. K. (ed.), *Railways and the Economic Development of Italy*, London: Macmillan.

2011, *The Reinterpretation of Italian Economic History*, Cambridge, Cambridge University Press.

Findlay R. and O'Rourke K. H., 2007, *Power and Plenty: Trade, War and the World Economy in the Second Millennium*, Princeton: Princeton University Press.

Fouquet R. and Broadberry S., 2015, "Seven Centuries of European Economic Growth and Decline," *Journal of Economic Perspectives*, 29 (4), pp. 227–244.

Francese M. and Pace A., 2008, "Il debito pubblico italiano dall'unità a oggi. Una ricostruzione storica," *Quaderni di Economia e Finanza*, 31, Rome: Bank of Italy.

Fuà G. (ed.), 1975, *Lo sviluppo economico in Italia, Vol 3, Studi di settore e documentazione di base*, Milano: Franco Angeli..

Fumagalli G., 1921, *Chi l'ha detto? Tesoro di citazioni italiane e straniere, di origine letteraria e storica*, Milan: Hoepli.

Galbraith K, 1958, *The Affluent Society*, Boston: Houghton Mifflin.

Gigliobianco A. and Giorgiantonio C., 2017, "Concorrenza e mercato nelle cultura," in Gigliobianco A. and Toniolo G. (eds.), *Concorrenza, mercato e crescita in Italia: il lungo periodo*, Marsilio, Venezia, pp. 151–198.

Gioberti V., 1845, *Del primato morale e civile degli italiani*, Lausanne, Bonamici & Co.

Giorgi C. and Pavan I., 2021, *Storia dello stato sociale in Italia*, Bologna: Mulino.

Gomellini M. and Toniolo G., 2017, "The Industrialization of Italy, 1861–1971," in O'Rourke K. H. and Williamson J. (eds.), *The Spread of Modern Industry to the Periphery since 1871*, Oxford and New York: Oxford University Press.

Graziani A., 1960), "Il commercio estero del Regno delle Due Sicilie dal 1832 al 1858," in Graziani, A. (ed.), *Archivio economico dell'unificazione italiana* 10 (1), Rome: Edindustria Editoriale.

Group of Ten, 2018, "International Capital Movements and Foreign Exchange Markets" www.bis.org/publ/gten_f.pdf.

Harrison M. and Galssi F., 2005, "Italy at War, 1915–18," in Harrison M. (ed.), *The Economics of World War I*, Cambridge: Cambridge University Press, pp. 276–309.

ISTAT, 1957, "Indagine statistica sullo sviluppo del reddito nazionale in Italia dal 1861 al 1956," *Annali di statistica*, VIII, Roma: ISTAT.

2011, *Report. Livelli di istruzione e partecipazione alla formazione*, Rome: ISTAT.

2016, *Le previsioni per l'economia italiana nel 2016*, Rome: ISTAT.

Iuzzolino G., Pellegrini G., Viesti G., 2013, "Regional convergence," in Toniolo G. (ed.), *The Oxford Handbook of the Italian Economy since Unification*, Oxford and New York: Oxford University Press, pp. 571–598.

Judt, T. 2010, *Postwar: A History of Europe since 1945*, London: Vintage.

Keynes J. M., 1923, *A Tract on Monetary Reform*, London: Macmillan.

Kindleberger C. P., 1996, *World Economic Primacy*, Oxford: Oxford University Press.

Kuznets S., 1966, *Modern Economic Growth*, New Haven, Yale University Press.

Maddison A., 2010, *Historical Statistics of the World Economy 1–2008 AD*, Paris: OECD.

Malanima P., 2003, *L'economia italiana: Dalla crescita medievale alla crescita contemporanea*. Bologna: Il Mulino.

Micossi S., 2017, "Storia breve degli interventi per la gestione delle crisi delle grandi imprese dagli anni Venti ad oggi," – XXIV Convegno Annuale dell'Associazione Albese degli Studi di Diritto Commerciale – Alba, 18 novembre.

Mounk Y., 2022, *The Great Experiment: Why Diverse Democracies Fall Apart and How They Can Endure*, London: Penguin Press.

North D. C. and Thomas R. P., 1973, *The Rise of the Western World. A New Economic History*, Cambridge: Cambridge University Press.

Onado M.: la Voce.info: www.lavoce.info/archives/13190/telecom-una-triste-storia-di-capitalismo-italiano/, 2013

Onado, M., 2014, *Alla ricerca della banca perduta*, Bologna: Il Mulino.

Padoan P. C., 2019, *Il sentiero stretto e oltre*, Bologna: Il Mulino

Pavan Ilaria, 2004, *Tra indifferenza e oblio. Le conseguenze economiche dell leggi razziali in Italia, 1938–1970*, Firenze: Le Monnier.

Pedani M. P., 2012, *Venezia e Suez 1504–2012*, Venice: Edizioni Ca' Foscari.

Romeo R., 1959, *Risorgimento e capitalismo*, Rome: Laterza.

Rossi N. and Toniolo G., 1996, "Italy," in Crafts N. and Toniolo G. (eds.) *Economic Growth in Europe since 1945*, Cambridge: Cambridge University Press, pp. 427–454.

Rossi S., 2007, *La politica economica italiana 1968–2007*, Rome: Laterza.

Salvati M., 2000, *Occasioni mancate. Economia e politica in Italia dagli anni '60 a oggi*, Rome: Laterza.

Saraceno P., 1963, *L'Italia verso la piena occupazione*, Milan: Feltrinelli.

Schivardi, F. and Schmitz, T., "The ICT Revolution and Italy's Two Lost Decades," Università Bocconi, EIEF and IGIER Università Bocconi.

Sereni E., 1971, *Il capitalismo nelle campagne (1860–1900)*, Turin: Einaudi.

Stone D., 2012, "Editor's Introduction: Postwar Europe as History," in Stone D. (ed.), *The Oxford Handbook of European History*, Oxford and New York: Oxford University Press, pp. 1–36.

Toniolo G., 1977, "Effective Protection and Industrial Growth: The Case of Italian Engineering (1898–1913)," *The Journal of European Economic History*, VI, pp. 659–73.

1980, *L'economia dell'Italia fascista*, Rome: Laterza.

1995, "Italian Banking, 1919–1939," in C. Feinstein (ed.), *Banking, Currency and Finance in Europe between the Wars*, Oxford: Clarendon Press, pp. 296–314.

2003, "La storia economica dell'Italia liberale: Una rivoluzione in atto," *Rivista di Storia Economica*, 2 (3), pp. 247–264.

(ed.), 2013, *The Oxford Handbook of the Italian Economy since Unification*, Oxford and New York: Oxford University Press.

2015, *An Economic History of Liberal Italy, 1850–1918*, 2nd edition, London and New York: Routledge Revivals.

2022, *Storia della Banca d'Italia: Tomo I, Origine e formazione di una banca centrale 1893–1943*, Rome: Laterza.

Toniolo G., Conte L. and Vecchi G., 2003, "Monetary Union, Institutions and Financial Market Integration: Italy 1862–1905," *Explorations in Economic History*, 40, pp. 443–461.

Toniolo G. , Vecchi G., 2007, "Italian Children at Work," *Il Giornale degli Economisti e Annali d'Economia*, 66, pp. 410–27.

Vecchi G., 2017, *Measuring Well Being: A History of Italian Living Standards*, Oxford and New York: Oxford University Press.

Visco I., 1995, "Inflation, Inflation Targeting and Monetary Policy: Notes for discussion on the Italian Experience," in Leidman L. e Svensson L.E.O (eds.), *Inflation Targets*, London: CEPR.

2014, *Investire in conoscenza*, Bologna: Il Mulino.

2018, *Anni difficili. Dalla crisi finanziaria alle nuove sfide per l'economia*, Bologna: Il Mulino.

Volker P. and Harper C., 2018, *Keeping at It: The Quest for Sound Monetary Policy and Good Government*, New York: Public Affairs.

Wolf M., 2022, "A Call to Arms for Diverse Democracies and Their Decent Middle," *The Financial Times*, May 5.

WTO, 1994, *Agreement on Trade-Related Aspects of Intellectual Property Rights*, Geneva: WTO.

Zamagni V., 1993, *Dalla periferia al centro. La seconda rinascita economica dell'Italia, 1861–1990*, Bologna: Il Mulino.

2007, *Introduzione alla storia economica d'Italia*, Bologna: Il Mulino.

Index

174

Index

Printed in the United States
by Baker & Taylor Publisher Services